35.00
60J

EXPERTS' CHOICE

EXPERTS'

CHOICE

1000 Years of the Art Trade

TEXT BY **John Walker**
DIRECTOR EMERITUS
THE NATIONAL GALLERY, WASHINGTON, D.C.

Stewart, Tabori & Chang, Publishers, New York

The works of art in this catalogue are arranged as nearly
as possible in chronological order, interrelating countries of
origin, styles, media, and so on.

In measurements, height precedes width and depth.

Information regarding the works of art has been provided
by each exhibitor. In most cases, the bibliographical data
have been checked against the sources, but neither C.I.N.O.A.
nor the Virginia Museum of Art is responsible for incorrect or
incomplete information.

Seventh International Exhibition Presented by
C.I.N.O.A.
La Confédération Internationale des Négociants en Oeuvres d'Art
The International Confederation of Art Dealers
at the Virginia Museum of Fine Arts,
Richmond, Virginia,
from April 22 to June 12, 1983

Design: Susan Wilson, Nai Chang
Editorial: Patricia Bayer, Susan E. Meyer

Library of Congress Cataloging in Publication Data

Walker, John, 1906 Dec. 24–
        Experts'choice.

        "Seventh international exhibition presented by C.I.N.O.A. . . .
Virginia Museum of Fine Arts, Richmond, Virginia."
        Bibliography: p.
        1. Art—Exhibitions.   2. Art—Collectors and collect-
ing—Exhibitions.   3. Art dealers—Exhibitions.
I. International Confederation of Dealers in Works of Art.
II. Title.
N8655.R5V579   1983   707'.4'0155451   82-19596
ISBN: 0-941434-31-1

Published in 1983 by Stewart, Tabori & Chang, Publishers, Inc., New York

Distributed by Workman Publishing Company, Inc.
1 West 39th Street, New York, New York 10018

Printed and bound in Japan.

CONTENTS

PREFACE

It gives me great pleasure to write this preface to the catalogue of the Seventh International C.I.N.O.A. Exhibition, "Experts' Choice." In October 1974, after many months of preparation, the previous C.I.N.O.A. show, "The Grand Gallery," opened to much acclaim at The Metropolitan Museum of Art in New York. The endeavor was monumental, the likes of which we thought would not happen again for quite a while. When members of the board and staff at the Virginia Museum confirmed interest in the International Confederation of Art Dealers' preparing an exhibition at their institution, however, there was no way to resist undertaking such a venture again. It is not only a great compliment to the art and antiques dealers, but it is the ultimate demonstration of cooperation between two vital factors in the world of art: the museum and the dealer.

It is not easy for an art dealer to commit a work of art to an exhibition more than a year in advance. The dealer must either put away the item, without showing it, or, if it is sold, the dealer must convince the new owner to lend it—being fully cognizant of the risks involved in having a painting or object transported and installed in a large exhibition. I am sure you will agree that the more-than-150 works of art from some eighty dealers in seven countries represent a first-rate cross-section of the art market today, illustrating the breadth and quality of what can be collected in the 1980s.

The art dealers taking part in this exhibition are among the most venerable and respected in the world; some of the firms have existed for well over a century. All belong to associations of dealers that in turn comprise La Confédération Internationale des Négociants en Oeuvres d'Art (C.I.N.O.A.), which was founded nearly fifty years ago in Belgium and today includes nineteen art and antiques dealer associations in thirteen countries. C.I.N.O.A.'s bylaws state that one of the organization's primary aims is "to encourage artistic development throughout the world." The organization has attemped to achieve this goal in several highly visible ways, including the mounting of major exhibitions such as this. Another method—established in 1976—has been the C.I.N.O.A. Prize, an award of $5,000, given annually to assist in the publication of an outstanding manuscript by a young or nonestablished art historian.

This exhibition and the catalogue that accompanies it illustrate the continuing importance of dealers in the art market. Their ability to assemble such a diverse collection of outstanding paintings and quality objects demonstrates both their dedication and their connoisseurship. We hope that you can appreciate these works of art in and of themselves—regardless of their ownership or monetary value. Art, after all, should be admired for its own sake.

On behalf of the International Confederation of Art Dealers, I would like to extend my thanks to the Virginia Museum of Fine Arts for presenting this exhibition in their beautiful and expanding institution. Special thanks go to Charles L. Reed, Jr., President of the Museum, and Margaret R. Burke, Deputy Director; to Pinkney L. Near, Chief Curator and Director of the Collections Division, and Richard B. Woodward, Curator of Exhibitions, who gave us great help in organizing the exhibition; and to all the Virginia Museum staff who aided considerably in bringing this show from the idea to the reality. In this regard, I would especially like to thank Mrs. Morgan Whitney, Fellow of the Virginia Museum, in whose mind's eye this exhibition appeared in the first place, and who then suggested it to us and to the Museum.

I am grateful to my fellow C.I.N.O.A. directors—Edward Munves, Jr., Vice President and former President of The National Antique & Art Dealers Association of America; David L. Dalva II, Secretary General and President of The Art and Antique Dealers League of America; Peter L. Schaffer, Treasurer and President of The National Antique & Art Dealers Association of America; and Stephen Hahn, Director and former President of the Art Dealers Association of America—for their constant encouragement, unflagging enthusiasm, and eager participation in this exhibition. In turn, our thanks go to the other dealers who have contributed to this exhibition —thus ensuring its success—by lending to the Virginia Museum this impressive array of works of art.

It may be difficult to imagine the complex task of organizing many dealers and works of art and then preparing a catalogue from so many descriptions prepared in varied formats, terminologies and languages! This task explains why I hesitated to embark on such a venture once again. Fortunately, we were extremely fortunate that Patricia Bayer, Projects Coordinator for C.I.N.O.A., agreed to put in so much time and effort to help make this exhibition and catalogue what they are. Diplomatically and enthusiastically, she acted as liaison between dealers and museum and worked unstintingly with the catalogue publisher as well.

This is by far the most beautiful and elaborate catalogue ever produced for a C.I.N.O.A. exhibition and in this regard we owe everything to Andrew Stewart, Susan E. Meyer, and Nai Chang, of Stewart, Tabori & Chang, without whose publishing, editing, and design expertise, respectively, this handsome catalogue would not have been produced.

Lastly, I join all those connected with this exhibition in thanking John Walker, Director Emeritus of the National Gallery of Art in Washington, D.C., who graciously consented to write the enlightening essay on the history of the art dealer for the catalogue. Despite a number of other writing commitments, Mr. Walker found the time to research and compose this essay, thus providing a fascinating and lively commentary to the illustrations of the works of art in this show.

Gerald G. Stiebel, President
La Confédération Internationale des
Négociants en Oeuvres d'Art

FOREWORD

It is a pleasure to recognize the members of C.I.N.O.A., La Confédération Internationale des Négociants en Oeuvres d'Art (The International Confederation of Art Dealers), and to host their exhibition, "Experts' Choice," at the Virginia Museum.

The realm of works of art that are "on the market" must become *terra cognita* to serious private collectors and curators in their endeavor to build, respectively, personal and public collections. In addition to providing an aesthetic treat for all viewers, the many fine works of art in the exhibition reveal something of this terrain and the potential delights that await the collector, and they aptly demonstrate the discerning judgment of the art dealers, who themselves play such an important role in the formation of collections.

An enjoyable and detailed panorama of the varied roles art dealers have assumed in history is admirably set forth in John Walker's essay in this catalogue. Director Emeritus of the National Gallery of Art in Washington, Mr. Walker is not only well qualified to write about the history of transactions in art, but he knows firsthand the important part that dealers —and donors—have played in the formation of museum collections during this century. His hope, expressed at the conclusion of his essay, that the human artistic heritage will continue to be preserved and enjoyed through enlightened collecting, is shared by the Virginia Museum, for the products of human creativity are precious and do not exist in inexhaustible or imperishable supply.

It is also to be hoped that exhibitions such as this will continue to be possible for a long time to come. And with this hope in mind, we join the Musée des Arts Décoratifs, Paris (1954), the Victoria and Albert Museum, London (1962), and The Metropolitan Museum of Art, New York (1974–1975), and others on the list of museums that have hosted the exhibitions organized by C.I.N.O.A. in the past.

Many people have helped make this exhibition possible, and special recognition must be given to Gerald Stiebel, President, Peter Schaffer, Treasurer, and Patricia Bayer, Projects Coordinator, for their work on behalf of C.I.N.O.A. in organizing the exhibition. To the many staff members of the Virginia Museum who have seen to the arrangements for the exhibition and accompanying programs in Richmond, special thanks are also extended.

Charles L. Reed, Jr., President
Virginia Museum

1000 Years of the Art Trade

John Walker

STANDING BUDDHA

Chinese, fifth–sixth century A.D.

Bronze, with greenish patination and traces of gilding; 11½ × 4 × 2¾″ (29 × 10 × 7 cm).

The figure's right hand is raised in abhaya mudrā and the left down in the gesture of varada mudrā.

SPINK & SON LTD., LONDON

1000 Years of the Art Trade

Trading in artifacts may not claim to be the world's oldest profession, but it is certainly among the oldest. To find its beginning, one would have to start looking at the dawn of civilization, because there have been artisans and patrons from earliest times. Thousands of years ago in Egypt, in Sumeria, in the Indus Valley, and in China, people exchanged treasures, but the transactions were directly between the fabricators—who were the artists—and the acquirers—who were the customers. Intermediaries—the dealers—came much later.

Until the third century B.C., there are few, if any, documented collectors as we know them. Patronage of works of art was motivated by religion or, in the case of portraiture, by vanity or homage. The acquisition of beautiful or historically important objects for their own sake does not appear in the West until very early in Hellenistic times (late fourth century B.C.) and in the East until the Han dynasty (third century B.C.) in China.

The first well-documented collector was King Attalus of Pergamum, although the early Ptolemies of Egypt may have preceded him. Pergamum was a small state on the western coast of Anatolia (now part of Turkey), and Attalus came to its throne in 241 B.C. He wished to make his capital, Pergamum, a principal center of Greek culture, and to this end he established a library rivaling the one created in Alexandria by the first Ptolemy. Attalus attracted the best artists of the time, and his Pergamene school became the most creative of all the Hellenistic schools of art. Attalus also wished to enrich Per-

gamum with as many masterpieces of Hellenic art as he could acquire. After his death he was followed by an art-collecting dynasty, Eumenes II and Attalus II and III, but in the end the Roman Empire swallowed up Pergamum.

From Greece, collecting spread to Rome. A major impetus was the sack of Corinth by the Romans in 146 B.C. When this ancient city was destroyed and its works of art looted, the Romans auctioned the spoils at one of the greatest sales in history. Prices reached unexpected heights. One painting of Dionysius by Aristides was bid up to 100 talents, a sum so large that the Roman general, Lucius Mummius, withdrew the picture from the auction and included it among the loot he dedicated in the Roman temples. When he learned its value, he much regretted that he had previously allowed his soldiers to use the panel as a table on which to throw dice. Even as generals go, he was exceptionally naïve about art. As Joseph Alsop points out in *The Rare Art Traditions*, Lucius Mummius warned the captain of the vessel carrying the trophies to Rome that if anything happened to the shipment, replacements would have to be provided. Such an order "was exactly like warning that identical replacements of Raphael or Leonardo would be demanded in case of damage when arranging air shipment of those pictures from Italy to the United States for one of the big museum shows."

In Rome naïveté about such matters disappeared quickly, and the art trade flourished. One dealer in particular became prominent, a Roman version

CONTINUED ON PAGE 14

11

◄ SEATED BUDDHA MAITREYA WITH TWO GUARDIAN DOGS

Chinese (probably from Lung-men), Northern Wei Dynasty, c. 520–525 A.D.

Dark grey limestone; 23⅞″ H (60.8 cm).

Similar examples: Fogg Art Museum, Cambridge, Massachusetts; Avery Brundage Collection, San Francisco; The Metropolitan Museum of Art, New York; Rijksmuseum, Amsterdam; Von der Heydt Collection, Museum Rietberg, Zürich.

RALPH M. CHAIT GALLERIES, INC., NEW YORK

BASIN ►

Chinese, T'ang Dynasty (618–907 A.D.).

Pottery, with vestiges of straw-yellow glaze; 3¾″ H, 9″ diam. (9.5, 23 cm).

Exhibitions: "Exhibition of Chinese Art," Venice, 1954, no. 341, ill. in cat.; "Arts of the T'ang Dynasty," Oriental Ceramic Society, London, 1955, no. 159, ill. in cat.

Provenance: George de Menasce, London.

This piece is derived from Chinese silver and bronze forms of the same period.

RALPH M. CHAIT GALLERIES, INC., NEW YORK

of the great early twentieth century dealer Lord Duveen. His name was Damasippus, and for a time he made a fortune, mostly peddling Greek Old Masters to Roman tycoons who were the equivalent of modern American millionaires. Cicero knew Damasippus and bought a group of Bacchantes from his shop. The orator later decided that this work was less suitable for a scholar than statues of the Muses were. The purchase was returned, and Damasippus, like many dealers today in similar circumstances, suffered a loss. In the end, this Greek precursor of modern art dealers went bankrupt. As Horace wrote, "Damasippus is mad in buying statues; the creditor of Damasippus, is he sound of mind?" The same might have been said of Duveen at one time.

Toward the end of the first century the poet Martial satirized a scene in the Saepta Julia (the Bond Street or the Fifty-seventh Street of Rome). The activities he describes are familiar to all art dealers: Mamurra, the central character, pretends to be a rich connoisseur. He enters several shops, considers a number of objects—pricing some, making insignificant offers on others, criticizing pieces of sculpture, and superciliously inspecting everything, even counting the emeralds in golden cups, weighing antique tankards, measuring a couch four times and then deciding it is too small. In the end, he buys only two slight cups for a penny.

Martial implies that Mamurra is much too poor to acquire any of the objects he had so patronizingly appraised. Nevertheless, this Roman dilettante had managed to pass an enjoyable morning, even though he had wasted the time of several dealers, an experience far from novel to the ladies and gentlemen whose works of art are in this very exhibition.

As the passion for collecting waxed, forgeries naturally followed. There is a touching letter from Pliny written in the first century A.D. He had just purchased a bronze of an old man in the realistic style popular in Hellenistic times. The piece was expensive, and Pliny had to use a legacy to buy it. At first, he was delighted with his purchase, but he then became anxious about its authenticity, and he admits his defective taste. He says the bronze "*appears* to be a genuine antique," but how can a mere novice be sure? The fear that his statuette may be a forgery seems to spoil his enjoyment, just as similar doubts have tarnished the delight of myriad collectors in the last 2,000 years. Nevertheless, Pliny orders a pedestal and decides to give his bronze to the Temple of Jupiter in his native province, where its authenticity may never be questioned.

Greco-Roman forgers were increasingly active, and today their skill still baffles curators. In the Metropolitan Museum of Art, for example, there is a small bronze horse that for years was labeled *Archaic Greek*. It seemed when I first saw it—and it still seems to me today—one of the most beautiful classical objects. Several years ago, a member of the museum staff declared the statue to be a modern fake. He was so sure of himself and offered such seemingly conclusive proof that the piece was withdrawn from exhibition. A few years later, after many technical and scientific tests had been performed, the horse was put back on exhibition labeled not *Archaic Greek* but *Hellenistic Copy*, an example of the brilliant forgeries done in Roman times.

Curators in ancient times probably encountered similar problems. They were priestly custodians, however, not scholarly experts, because the first art galleries were temples where all sorts of treasures—primarily votive offerings dedicated to the gods—were accumulated. Many of these donations were displayed in the sacred enclosure, which must have looked not unlike a modern sculpture garden. The more important temples were run by several officials who were responsible for inventories of the temple's possessions and for handing these posses-

TOMB FIGURE OF A DIGNITARY
(MING-CH'I)

Chinese, T'ang Dynasty (618–907 A.D.).

Glazed pottery; 40¼" H (102 cm).

Similar examples: The Metropolitan
   Museum of Art, New York; Tokyo
   National Museum; Los Angeles
   County Museum.

**E & J FRANKEL ORIENTAL ART,
NEW YORK**

BODHISATTVA MAITREYA

Cambodian (Buriram Province, Pra-kon Chai), eighth–ninth century A.D.

Bronze, with inlaid eyes; 21⅝″ H (55 cm).

Literature: Hugo Munsterberg, *Art of India and Southeast Asia*, New York, 1970, p. 232; E. C. Bunker, "Pre-Angkor Period Bronzes from Pra Kon Chai," Archives of Asian Art, vol. 25, 1971–1972, pp. 67–76, fig. 24.

Exhibition: "The Sensuous Immortals," Los Angeles County Museum of Art, 1977–1978, pl. 128 in cat.

Provenance: Ex-Pan Asian collection.

This figure of the future Buddha holds his right hand in the gesture of teaching, while his left hand may have held a pot.

R. H. ELLSWORTH, LTD., NEW YORK

sions on to their successors. They also acted as guides, since these shrines were visited much as museums are today.

In *Mime IV* of Herodas, there is a description of a visit by two women to the temple of Asklepios in Kos. These women must have been of modest means, because, with many apologies, they gave only a single cock as their offering. They go on to discuss the works of art that are on view, and they talk about Praxiteles and Apelles in the most knowing way, demonstrating that an appreciation of the early masters had filtered down to all classes, much as it has in modern times. One of the visitors says of Apelles, "May he who looks on him or on his works without the respect they merit be hung up like an old cloak in a fuller's shop."

A true public art gallery, not a temple, was developed at Sicyon, in southern Greece, and flourished until 56 B.C., when all the pictures were sold and brought to Rome to liquidate the public debt. There was also the Pinacotheca in the Propylaea of the Acropolis in Athens; the exact date when it became a picture gallery is uncertain, but by the second century A.D., it had become a museum and was visited by Pausanias. The public art galleries in Rome come closest to being the prototypes of our modern museums; the notion that great works of art should be accessible to all was Roman. Cicero advocates public galleries in one of his orations against Gaius Verres, who was such a passionate collector that when Mark Antony ordered him to surrender his beloved Corinthian bronzes, he refused, was proscribed, and died.

According to Pliny, Marcus Vipsanius Agrippa, the chief minister of Augustus, "held that great pictures and statues should become public property instead of being hidden in the villas of rich collectors." Under such pressure, many affluent Romans opened their houses to the public on certain days. To satisfy the mounting interest in art, the Baths of Agrippa were designed not only for bathing but also for displaying art. They were constantly enriched with new and beautiful acquisitions. The increasing attention given to art led to a fear that too many artistic treasures were being exported from Rome. During the first century A.D., plans were promulgated to nationalize the greatest masterpieces in order to stop the shipment of works of art to distant colonies. It is evident, therefore, that export restrictions are not new: dealers were hampered by them 2,000 years ago.

Nevertheless, there was one great difference between such protomuseums and those we know today. In the twentieth century, art dealing—as we shall see—affects the nature of both public and private collections. In Greek and Roman times, religious donations, combined with the booty of conquest, created public galleries. Art dealers existed, but they were far less influential than they have been in the last 300 years.

After the sixth century, art dealing ended, except for a limited market in Byzantium. For centuries, during the Dark and Middle Ages, art dealers were nonexistent in the West. With the Renaissance, they reappeared, mainly as commission agents at first, but gradually as an important element in Western culture.

FRANCESCO MAZZOLA, known as PARMIGIANINO (1503–1540)

The Emperor Charles V Receiving the World

Italian, c. 1529–1530.

Oil on canvas; 68 × 47″ (173 × 119.5 cm).

Literature: S. J. Freedberg, *Parmigianino, His Works in Painting*, Cambridge, Mass., 1950, pp. 207–208, fig. 134 (as copy)—recognized as original by Prof. Freedberg after cleaning and removal of earlier overpainting; Ferdinando Bologna, "Il 'Carlo V' del Parmigianino," *Paragone*, 1956; Maurizio Fagiolo dell'Arco, *Il Parmigianino*, Rome, 1970, pp. 270–271, no. 32, ills. 195, 285, 291; A. E. Popham, *Catalogue of Drawings of Parmigianino*, 3 vols., New Haven, 1971. Published for The Pierpont Morgan Library, The Franklin Jasper Walls Lectures. This painting mentioned under the entry for the drawing no. 318 and ill. pl. 234; Rosenberg & Stiebel, Inc., New York, *European Works of Art II*, 1979–1980, pp. 10–11; Paolo Rossi, *L'Opera Completa del Parmigianino*, Milan, 1980, no. 42, ill.

Exhibitions: "Major Masters of the Renaissance," The Rose Art Museum, Brandeis University, 1963, cat. no. 14; "Sixteenth Century Paintings from American Collections," Vassar College Art Gallery, 1964, no. 11; "Masters of the Portrait," The Oklahoma Museum of Art, Oklahoma City, 1979, no. 1.

Provenance: Cardinal Ippolita de Medici; Cardinal Ercole Gonzaga; The Dukes of Mantua (until at least 1630); William Angerstein, London; Lesser; Sir Francis and Sir Herbert Cook, Richmond, England (Catalogue London, 1932, no. 97).

The painting of this portrait, which was left unfinished by this Bolognese artist, is recorded by Vasari. Charles V was in Bologna to be crowned Holy Roman Emperor by Clement VII, thus cementing the Hapsburg rule over TRIA, Burgundy, The Netherlands, and Spain. There is a preliminary drawing for this painting in The Pierpont Morgan Library, New York.

ROSENBERG & STIEBEL, INC., NEW YORK

MIDDLE AGES AND RENAISSANCE

The Renaissance represented a break with the immediate past of the Middle Ages. It produced a new veneration for a more remote time, for the ancient world. First in Italy and then throughout Europe, this obsession with Greece and Rome caused spiritual, intellectual, and economic upheaval. As men turned back to the thoughts and values of antiquity, ego was reborn, personality was exalted, and the individual was glorified. Although artists held a new place in popular esteem as early as the fourteenth century, art dealing for contemporary work remained infrequent. Art sales were principally of classical objects. For these, there were passionate collectors everywhere.

Among the first was Oliviero Forzetta, a money-lender of Treviso, in northeastern Italy, whose collecting activities are worth examining. We have a memorandum, dated 1335, that gives us some idea of the works of art he wished to assemble, a kind of shopping list. More interesting than the objects themselves are the *sources* of his acquisitions and the absence of agents. He intends to journey to Venice to buy books to complete his classical library and to acquire ancient cameos, medals, and coins. No intermediary is involved; he plans to go directly to the owners. This was also true of another collector, Marino Falieri, a doge executed for treason in 1355. Among his treasures were two Hellenistic busts of Negroes brought from Africa. These he acquired without an intermediary, as far as we know, from a sailor named Jacobellus. Agents were often used, but when possible all collectors tried to avoid middlemen.

Forzetta was a pioneer among Renaissance collectors, but assemblages of coins, gems, and statues had been made in the late Middle Ages. In the first half of the thirteenth century, Holy Roman Emperor Frederick II gathered both coins and sculpture, the former as models for his own coinage and the latter to adorn his castle. At an even earlier date, in the twelfth century, Henry of Blois brought together a collection of classical art that he took from Rome to England, whence it has since vanished. But these two isolated cases were not enough to stimulate art dealing.

Toward the end of the fourteenth century, however, some art dealers put in a tentative appearance. They principally sold small devotional pictures made to adorn altars in private houses and to accompany travellers on their journeys. We even know of a Florentine wool merchant, Benedetto di Banco degli Albizzi, who specialized in such sales. His agents abroad were represented by the firm of Francesco di Marco Danti, whose principal market was at Avignon. (It is amusing to note that dealers in the fourteenth century marked up their wares by at least 100 percent, not very different from twentieth-century practice. But while the problems today are overhead, insurance, and lawsuits, the fourteenth-century dealer had to cover himself for hazardous journeys, taxes, and toll duties.) Danti's trade was mostly in mediocre objects, but he was willing to import better works of art when they were ordered in advance. He wanted his Florentine partners, however, to concentrate on reasonably priced pictures and, as he wrote, to buy "only when the

CONTINUED ON PAGE 28

SEDES SAPIENTIAE (THRONE OF WISDOM)

Liège or Mosan, c. 1230.

Boxwood; 17½ × 7 × 6½″ (44 × 18 × 16 cm).

JAN DIRVEN, EINDHOVEN

HEAD OF A BODHISATTVA OR KUAN YIN

Chinese, Yüan Dynasty (1280–1367 A.D.).

Stone; 22½ × 14 × 12″ (57 × 35.5 × 30 cm).

Exhibition: Biennale des Antiquaires, Paris, September-October 1980.

Similar examples: Musée Guimet, Paris; Von der Heydt Collection, Museum Rietberg, Zürich.

GALERIE JACQUES BARRÈRE, PARIS

BOWL

German (Rhineland), twelfth century, Romanesque.

Engraved with Latin names and allegorical representations of the Seven Vices. At the center is *Superbia*, or "Pride."

Bronze; 12″ diam. (30 cm).

Hand-washing vessels such as this were used in pairs by priests in the medieval liturgy (the companion piece to this bowl would have been decorated with the Seven Virtues).

OTTO SCHMITT KUNST & ANTIQUITÄTEN, COLOGNE

BELT BUCKLE AND TONGUE

French (Paris or Avignon), second quarter of the fourteenth century.

Chased silver, with insets of translucent enamel on silver; buckle length: 4¾" (12 cm); tongue length: 5½" (14 cm).

Literature: Rosenberg & Stiebel, Inc., New York, *European Works of Art III*, 1981, pp. 62–63.

Exhibition: "The Secular Spirit: Life and Art at the End of the Middle Ages," The Metropolitan Museum of Art, New York, 1975, p. 78, cat. no. 83, ill.

Provenance: Mr. and Mrs. Ernest Brummer, New York.

The girdle of this belt, which no longer survives, was probably made of leather or silk. The belt was worn loosely around the waist, with the tongue hanging down the front.

ROSENBERG & STIEBEL, INC., NEW YORK

PAIR OF ANGELS HOLDING CANDLESTICKS

German (Swabia), c. 1470, late Gothic.

Maker's mark on base of one angel.

Limewood; 26″ H (66 cm).

Literature: Julius Baum, "Die Samm-lung Dr. Oertel," *Der Cicerone V*, 1913, p. 280; Theodor Demmler, *Sammlung Dr. Oertel München*, Katalog der Auktion bei Rudolph Lepke, Berlin, 1913, nos. 59–60; "Sammlung Dr. Oertel München, Ergebnisliste der Versteigerung vom 6/7 Mai 1913," *Der Kunstmarkt X*, 1912/13, p. 283.

Provenance: Dr. Richard Oertel, Munich.

JAN DIRVEN, EINDHOVEN

ST. ANN WITH VIRGIN AND CHILD

German (Cologne), c. 1500, late Gothic.

Tilman van der Burch, sculptor.

Oak; 49 × 23½" (124.5 × 60 cm).

Similar example: See *Die Bildwerke der Fürstlich Hohenzollernschen Sammlung Sigmaringen*, Stuttgart and Zürich, 1925, pl. 39.

NEUSE-ANTIQUITÄTEN, BREMEN

FEMALE SAINT

French, end of the fifteenth century.

Attributed to the Master of Monesties (Albi region).

Painted wood (polychromy of the period); 58½ × 17½ × 15½″ (148 × 45 × 40 cm).

Provenance: Private collection, France.

BRESSET, PARIS

SEATED VIRGIN AND CHILD

South German, c. 1500, late Gothic.

Wood, carved and painted; 40″ H (102 cm).

Exhibition: "Alter Kunst aus dem Besitz Rheinhessischer, Mainzer, und ehemals Kurmainzer Familien," Mainz, 1925, no. 27.

Provenance: Georg Hirth, Munich (Auktion Helbing, November 28, 1916, no. 410); Marx collection, Mainz (Auktion Helbing, December 6, 1927, no. 90).

NEUSE-ANTIQUITÄTEN, BREMEN

master who makes them is in need." Over the centuries, nothing has greatly changed.

In the fifteenth century, artists themselves were dealers. According to Ulrich Middeldorf, a commercial painter named Neri di Bicci, an excellent craftsman, ordered fifty-five stucco reliefs from Desiderio da Settignano. These he polychromed, framed, and sold quickly to enjoy a brisk and profitable business. Artists also seem to have painted pictures for stock. In Venice, one could undoubtedly purchase a ready-made Madonna and Child signed *Giovanni Bellini* from the painter. Later, in the sixteenth century, Titian and others appear to have had many paintings on hand for sale.

In the Quattrocento, however, with a few exceptions such as those mentioned above, the professional art dealer was still a commission agent rather than a dealer with a shop and a stock of paintings or sculpture ready for sale. For such an investment, usury made the necessary capital excessively expensive. In the fifteenth century, an Italian dealer's job was to find specimens of ancient art—if that was what his client wanted—or to negotiate with other collectors, or more rarely with artists, for their own work. Direct patronage took care of the rest.

The leading collectors who used agents to buy classical works of art were the Florentine humanists to whom we owe the recovery of so many classical texts. Except for the greatest of all, Cosimo de' Medici, they were not rich men. Niccolò Niccoli, who was probably the leader of these lovers of antiquity, ran through a large fortune purchasing classical art and texts; on his death he owed the Medici bank 500 ducats, a large sum in those days. Another enthusiast was Poggio Bracciolini, who was a protégé of Niccolò Niccoli and became chancellor of Florence. These and other collectors used as "runners" men like Fra Francesco da Pistoia, a Minorite friar who spent much of his time in Greece and the Aegean Islands. In the course of his travels, he came across a Greek called Suffretus who had a large number of antiquities. Fra Francesco brought this collection to Poggio's attention. Naturally the friar expected a commission as a "finder," as well as one for buying items from his Greek friend. But Poggio thought—as collectors often have—that he could outsmart his agent, and he negotiated directly with Suffretus. Eventually, however, the friar was able to take his revenge; when he was acting as the shipper of a larger and more valuable consignment for Poggio from another classical collector, he delivered the shipment instead to Cosimo de' Medici. Although Poggio was apoplectic with fury, he was unable to recover his purchases.

There were other traders in antiquities, such as Ciriaco d'Ancona. A greatly respected scholar, Ciriaco was received with honor by all his fellow humanists and collectors when he visited Florence on a political mission. His survey of the most important classical collections then to be seen in Florence, as recounted by his friend Scalamonti, offers an idea of the richness of Florentine collecting. Treasures were to be found not only in the houses of the aristocracy, but also in those of artists such as Donatello, Ghiberti, and Verrocchio. These sculptors also acted as experts and restorers for the richer Florentines. Even Leonardo da Vinci counseled Isabella d'Este about buying some precious vessels available from Lorenzo de' Medici's collection, but she seems to have ignored Leonardo's advice.

Collections were not limited to antiquities. All over Italy, but especially in Florence, there were many collectors of contemporary art. In gathering modern pictures and statues, agents were rarely used, except when the artist was in another city. There was a close relationship between the wealthy and the painters and sculptors. Transactions were a matter of patronage, not of purchase.

As the sixteenth century progressed and collecting increased, art dealers in the modern sense became more significant. Among the first of these was Giovanni Battista della Porta, an opponent of

CONTINUED ON PAGE 32

UNKNOWN ARTIST

The Burial of Christ with Figures of Donors.

Netherlandish, middle of the sixteenth century.

Oil on wood; 6¼ × 25½″ (16 × 65 cm).

This painting is a predella from an altarpiece.

WOLFGANG A. SIEDLER, VIENNA

RAFFAELLO SANZIO DA URBINO, known as RAPHAEL (1483–1520)

Saint Mary Magdalene

Italian, c. 1503.

Tempera and oil on poplar panel; 15 × 5½" (38.2 × 14 cm).

Reverse painted to simulate varicolored marble, and with following Latin inscription at center: BENEDI   NOS C
CAT VIRG   UM PRO
O MARIA   LE PIA

(Translation: May the Virgin Mary bless us with her holy offspring.)

Literature: Oskar Fischel: "Some Lost Drawings By or Near to Raphael," *The Burlington Magazine*, no. CVII, vol. XX, February 1912, pp. 294–300, pls. 2–3; *Raffaels Zeichnungen*, Berlin 1913–1914, pp. 70, 71, 73, pl. 63; and "Raffaels heilige Magdalene im Berliner kgl. Kupferstichkabinett," *Jahrbuch der Königlich Preussischen Kunstsammlungen*, vol. 36, 1915, pp. 92–96, pl. 2; Georg Gronau, *Raffael, des Meisters Gemälde* (Klassiker der Kunst), Berlin, 1922, pl. 20, pp. 223, 253; Wolfgang Schöne, "Raphaels Kronung des heiligen Nikolaus von Tolentino," in *Eine Gabe der freunde für Carl George Heise Zum 28.VI.1950*, p. 136, no. 43; Roberto Longhi, "Percorso di Raffaello Giovine," *Paragone*, May 1955, p. 22; Ettore Camesasca, *Tutta la pitture di Raffaello*, I, Milan, 1956, p. 81; Oskar Fischel, *Raphael*, Berlin, 1962, fig. 24; Pier Luigi de Vecchi, *L'opera completa di Raffaello*, Milan, 1966, p. 91, no. 30; Bernard Berenson, *Italian Pictures of the Renaissance, Central Italian and North Italian Schools*, London, 1968, vol. I, p. 352; Luitpold Dussler, *Raphael, A Critical Catalogue of His Pictures, Wall-Paintings, and Tapestries*, New York, 1971 (Munich, 1966), p. 16, pls. 36, 37.

Provenance: Count Alessandro Contini-Bonacossi, Florence (acquired in the 1930s)

The painting is one of a pair; on the other panel, which is in a private collection, is represented Saint Catherine of Alexandria (in most cases, literature cited above refers to both works). The two paintings were probably the side panels of a triptych.

Preparatory drawings exist for both works. The drawing for Saint Mary Magdalene (measuring approximately 12 × 3¾", or 30.2 × 9.5 cm) is in the Collection Kupferstichkabinett, Dahlem Museum, West Berlin. As with the Saint Catherine drawing, the figure is identical in size to the painted one, its outline pricked for transfer onto the prepared gesso panel. In addition, examination of *Saint Mary Magdalene* by the infra-red ray Vitecon camera has revealed prickings on the underlying gesso, consistent with those in the Berlin drawing.

SPENCER A. SAMUELS & COMPANY, LTD., NEW YORK

BAREND VAN ORLEY (1492–1542)

Crucifixion on Mount Calvary

Flemish, c. 1530.

Oil on panel; 55 × 51″ (140 × 130 cm).

Literature: Paul Clemen, *Die Kunst-denkmäler der Rheinprovinz*, vol. X, III, Aachen, Profandenkmäler und Sammlungen, 1924, p. 257, fig. 133.

Exhibition: Westfälisches Landes-museum, Münster, 1975–1976.

Provenance: Zanoli, Cologne, 1850; Franziska Clavé-Bouhaben, née Zanoli, Cologne, 1894; Theodor Nellessen, Aachen, 1927.

At right are depicted the donor and his coat of arms, that of the Hamburg family of Miles (de Ridder).

H. G. KLEIN, COLOGNE

the Medici who flourished during their eclipse but fled to France and made many friends at court there after the Medici returned from exile. In 1527, when the Medici were again expelled, della Porta hastened back to Florence, bearing with him commissions from Francis I. He ordered works of art for the king, including sculpture from Tribolo for the palace at Fontainebleau, and he commissioned some paintings and sculptures on his own. Della Porta was handicapped by the fact that artists did not produce their work directly for dealers as they do today. If artists painted for stock, they sold their pictures or statues themselves. Dealers were thus confined to commissions awarded as private speculation, or to the work of major Renaissance artists who might come on the market due to of the constantly shifting fortunes of the nobility, or, above all, to the sale of classical antiquities.

Even with these limitations, one important dealer did arise: Jacopo da Strada. Born in Mantua in 1507 and trained as a goldsmith, he lived in several countries, like many dealers do today. He was a citizen of Nuremberg, resided in Vienna, and was active for long periods in Venice and Rome. His portrait, painted by Titian, shows him as a person of consequence, seated at a table strewn with medals and coins and holding a statue of Venus. At first, his principal sales were to the Fuggers of Augsburg. They kept part of what they bought for their castle in Kirchheim; the rest they unloaded on various princely families at considerable profit. Strada's principal Fugger patron was Johann Jakob, who had the unusual misfortune among the Fuggers of becoming bankrupt. But Strada was then lucky enough to be taken on as an expert by the Duke of Bavaria, later one of Strada's best clients.

In search of antiquities, Strada went to Rome, entered the services of Pope Julius III, and was given the title *Civis Romanus*, which he greatly prized. He returned to Nuremberg and, through Ferdinand of Tirol, gained access to the court of

the Hapsburgs. Forgeries were everywhere, and Strada had a reputation for his keen eye. He settled down in Vienna for a time and advised Emperor Maximilian II. When Duke Albrecht V of Bavaria wanted to build an Antiquarium attached to the Residence at Munich, he requested Strada to be his architect and agent in order to help him gather the collection he intended to form. Strada bought for him widely if not wisely, at least judging by what we see today. Many of the pieces of classical sculpture in the collection are overrestored, and there are numerous fakes. But these dubious statues cost the duke 21,940 gulden, a huge sum spent in a short time by his agent. There exists a letter from Cardinal Otto von Augsburg, warning the duke that Strada was dishonest and that he, the cardinal, could enrich the ducal Antiquarium with better antiquities for less money. But Strada, like Duveen, had a personality that rose above such scandalous allegations. Strada retained the ducal favor, in spite of the cardinal's claim that the moment Strada came to Rome, the dealers raised their prices accordingly. The cardinal's offer to find "honorable people" went unheard.

In the sixteenth century, dealers sometimes bought with partners in order to be able to make larger purchases, as they occasionally do today. One of these partnerships was centered around Strada. A member of his group, Carlo della Serpa, owned a jeweled casket, which Strada offered to the duke for 1,000 ducats. The duke agreed to the purchase provided the casket met his approval after he inspected it. The duke refused, however, to be responsible for its transport. The partners suggested that Titian, a part-owner, send the casket to Bavaria at his own risk. The painter declined, and as there were no insurance companies the problem seemed insoluble. Then a man called David Ott volunteered to become an underwriter, so to speak, presumably for a fee. When the purchase was finally consummated, all the partners profited handsomely.

CONTINUED ON PAGE 39

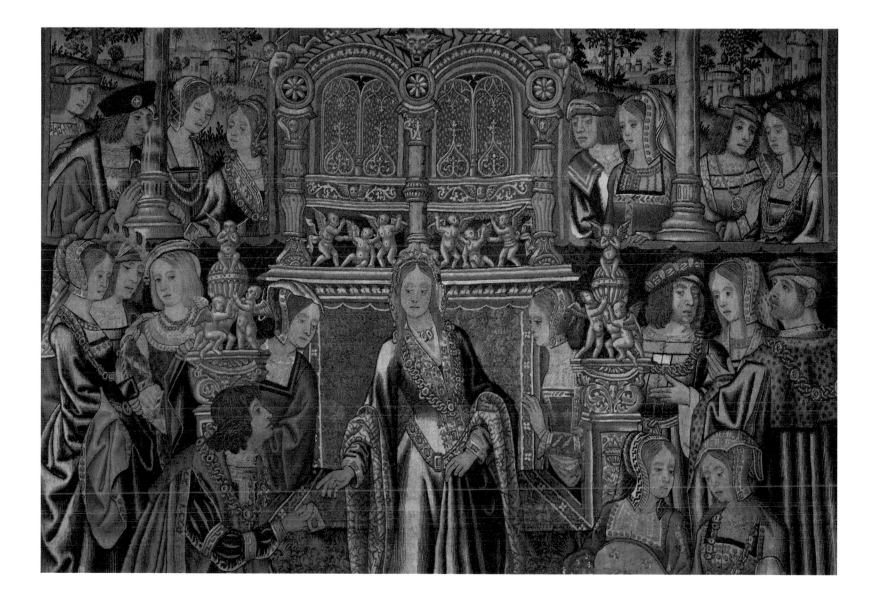

TAPESTRY

Saint Ursula Receiving the Ambassadors

Flemish (Tournai?), second quarter of the sixteenth century.

Wool (fragment); 72 × 106″ (183 × 269 cm).

VOJTECH BLAU INC., NEW YORK

**FRANS POURBUS THE ELDER
(1545–1581)**

Portrait of a Boy

Flemish, 1573.

Dated, at left: ANNO DNI 1573.

Age of sitter, at right: AETATIS SVAE 3.

Annotation, on back: "Fils de
l'Empereur."

Oil on panel; 6¾″ diam. (17.5 cm).

Exhibitions: "Le Portrait dans les Anciens Pays-Bas," Musée Communal,
Bruges, 1953, p. 75, no. 122, ill.;
"Le Siècle de Brueghel," Musées
Royaux des Beaux-Arts de Belgique, Brussels, 1963, no. 200,
fig. 242.

Provenance: Beets & Fontein,
Amsterdam, 1929; H. Smidt van
Gelder, Overveen, The Nether-
lands (since 1929).

One of a pair, see painting at right.

**GALERIE HOOGSTEDER B.V.,
THE HAGUE**

FRANS POURBUS THE ELDER
(1545–1581)

Portrait of a Girl

Flemish, 1573.

Dated, at left: ANNO DNI 1573.

Age of sitter, at right: AETATIS SVAE 5.

Annotation, on back: "Fille l'ainée de l'Empereur."

Oil on panel; 6¾″ diam. (17.5 cm).

Exhibitions: "Le Portrait dans les Anciens Pays-Bas," Musée Communal, Bruges, 1953, p. 75, no. 123, ill.; "Le Siècle de Brueghel," Musées Royaux des Beaux-Arts de Belgique, Brussels, 1963, no. 201, fig. 243.

Provenance: Beets & Fontein, Amsterdam, 1929; H. Smidt van Gelder, Overveen, The Netherlands (since 1929).

One of a pair, see painting at left.

GALERIE HOOGSTEDER B.V., THE HAGUE

PLATTER

French (Limoges), second half of the sixteenth century.

Jean de Court (active 1555–1585), maker.

Enamelled copper; 23¾″ W (60.5 cm).

Provenance: Seligman collection, Paris, 1920s.

Three episodes from the story of the rape of Europa are depicted on the front of the platter; the back is decorated with masks and half-figures typical of the Renaissance period.

BLUMKA GALLERY, NEW YORK

GOBLET

English (London), 1570, Elizabeth I.

William Dyxson, maker; hallmarks for London 1570.

Silver; 7″ H (18 cm); weight: 8½ oz.

Literature: J. B. Carrington and G. R. Hughes, *The Plate of the Worshipful Company of Goldsmiths*, Oxford, 1926, pl. no. 24, no. 6.

Provenance: The Worshipful Company of Goldsmiths, London.

JAMES ROBINSON INC., NEW YORK

JUG

Turkish/English

Turkish (Isnik) jug, painted earthenware, c. 1585

English mount, silver-gilt, c. 1585

10½″ H (26.7 cm); in fitted case.

Provenance: The Lord St. Oswell MC,
  Nostell Priory, Wakefield,
  Yorkshire.

**RONALD A. LEE (FINE ARTS)
LTD., LONDON**

In spite of the happy ending, this incident illustrates the difficulties Renaissance art dealers faced because of the lack of insurance and the risk of transport.

Over the years, Strada became a very rich man. Although Cardinal von Augsburg may have stated that Strada's integrity was not above question, the dealer was—like Duveen—ennobled. His home in Vienna contained many marble statues and a library of more than 3,000 volumes. He married into the aristocracy, and one of his daughters had the honor of becoming the mistress of the Emperor Rudolph II and bearing him six children. When Strada left the imperial service in 1579, he received a final accolade: his son was appointed by Rudolph to be the next court antiquary. Thus the first important art dealer who was a consummate courtier (as art dealers should be) ended his life honored and admired in Vienna.

In the Netherlands during this period, the history of art dealing and collecting was somewhat different. The art and craft guilds were all-powerful, and their edicts were strictly enforced. Tapestries and *objets d'art* were more highly prized than paintings. When Marguerite de Lannoy died, for example, her pictures were bequeathed to members of her household, while her noble relations received manuscripts and jewels. Middle-class families usually had at least one devotional picture, those on linen being more popular and less expensive than those on panel. Woven wall hangings, however, were the most sought after. It has been estimated that 4½ percent of all Netherlandish exports were tapestries.

Nearly all artists were subject to the guilds, which maintained monopolies, restricted competition, and for a time saw to it that only painters operated as dealers. The dues required by the guilds varied and depended on fenestration: artists who occupied windowless shops paid less than did those whose studios contained shop windows. The guilds also controlled the supply of paint and kept down the prices of artist's materials. But, most significant, they forbade the importation of artworks, except for those pieces shown at the great fairs in Antwerp, Ghent, and elsewhere in the region. Sanctioned by civil authorities, these guild regulations, if broken, could be prosecuted in civil courts.

Unlike in Italy, only a small number of works of art were commissioned. Most were chosen by the patron from the artist's or dealer's stock. Painters relied on their shop windows for their sales. Clients would choose from what they saw or from models that would be repeated.

The activities of dealers in the Netherlands remain somewhat mysterious. For example, in 1445, Alfonso V of Aragon procured a panel by Van Eyck from a Valencian merchant, but how it reached Spain is unknown. The Medici and the Estes used their representatives to purchase works of art, but whether they bought from dealers or directly from artists is uncertain, although probably both sources were used. We know that the Medici bank at Bruges placed orders for tapestries, usually at Lille, for their customers, but we do not know whether dealers were involved.

By the sixteenth century, Netherlandish pictures flooded the Italian market. The Duke of Mantua, for instance, acquired from one Mattheo de Nasar, a dealer, 120 Flemish paintings in a single transaction. Most of the pictures on the art market were created by living artists from the north, but dealers also occasionally supplied Old Masters. This would happen, however, only when a church would be willing to sell an altarpiece or when a noble family would release a painting. With time, the guilds relaxed their restrictions on sales and accepted the existence of dealers. In the end, in spite of the prejudice against them, a few dealers were even permitted to become guild members. Later in the sixteenth century, the guilds' authority diminished, and in the seventeenth century their principal role was to maintain standards of craftsmanship.

MATHIEU LE NAIN (1607–1677)

The Fife Player

French, 1660s.

Oil on canvas; 37 × 47¼″
(94 × 120 cm).

Literature: Catalogue of LeNain
Exhibition, Petit Palais, Paris, 1934,
no. 47; George Isarlo, "Les trois
LeNain et leur suite," *La Renaissance*, March 1938, pl. 57; Jacques
Thuillier, *Les Frères LeNain*, Paris,
1978–1979, p. 323 (exhib. cat.).

Exhibition: LeNain Exhibition, Petit
Palais, Paris, 1934, no. 47.

Provenance: George Wilbraham, 1930.

**BERNARD HOUTHAKKER C.V.,
AMSTERDAM**

SEVENTEENTH CENTURY

With the seventeenth century, art collecting ascended to princely heights—aided not by rulers alone, but also by those with princely revenues. Italy was entering a period of economic decline, and the agents of collectors in England, France, the Netherlands, Austria, and Germany swarmed across the Alps with golden hooks to draw masterpieces from palazzos and villas. They received their funds from the leaders of Europe: Philip IV of Spain, Cardinal Richelieu and Cardinal Mazarin in France, Archduke Leopold Wilhelm of Hapsburg, and, above all, Charles I of England.

The collection of Charles I is worth examining in some detail, since it is probably the finest ever formed by an individual. He began to collect in 1616, when he was Prince of Wales, and he continued to collect for twenty-four years, until Parliament refused him sufficient resources. In 1648, the Commonwealth began to disperse his collection, selling even his personal and hereditary possessions. There has never been a sale of comparable magnitude, except the dispersal of the treasures of Versailles, also the product of revolution.

Charles I's most important agent was Daniel Nys, who negotiated the purchase of the entire Gonzaga collection, a fantastic coup, and sold his own stock of pictures to the king. From Nys and other sources, Charles ended up with two dozen Titians. He purchased more works by Titian than by any of the other great Renaissance masters—more even than works of Van Dyck, his own court painter, from whom he only acquired about a dozen. (His judg-ment was good. Titian was by far the greater artist.) The king wanted every important Renaissance painter represented in his collection. When the sale of his collection began, Charles owned nearly 1,400 pictures and 400 pieces of sculpture. His curator, Abraham van der Dort, made an inventory and included whatever provenances he could ascertain. Furthermore, he noted the condition of the paintings, and the words (familiar to dealers and curators today) "damaged," "overwashed," and "scoured" often appear on his list. The harm that sometimes can be done to works of art by restorers has not been limited to this century!

Although the collection of Charles I may have been the greatest in the world, there were many English peers who were equally avid collectors. The Earl of Arundel, for example, had agents on the Continent, in Mediterranean lands, and as far east as Turkey. His collection of ancient art at Arundel House was a pilgrimage site for those fortunate enough to see it. Arundel's great rival as a collector was the Duke of Buckingham, whose beauty made him the favorite of James I and Charles I, James's son. Both monarchs loaded him with honors and awards, making it possible for him to fill his huge mansion, York House, with works of art. Then there was a third immensely rich collector, the Earl of Pembroke, in the king's circle. This triumvirate of collectors made seventeenth-century London the lodestone for dealers that New York has been in the twentieth century.

Paintings were not the only treasures that poured

CONTINUED ON PAGE 45

HOUSE ALTAR

German (Augsburg), c. 1600.

Matthias Wallbaum (1554–1632), maker.

Silver, ebony; 28½ × 18 × 5″ (73 × 46 × 13 cm).

Literature: Dr. Regina Löwe, *Die Augsburger Goldschmiedewerkstatt des Matthias Walbaum*, Munich, Baye-rischen Nationalmuseum, 1975, cf. p. 28, fig. 5; Helmut Seling, *Die Kunst der Augsburger Goldschmiede 1529–1868*, Munich, 1980, vol. I, pp. 56–57; vol. II, p. 47.

Exhibition: Schnütgen Museum, Co-logne, 1977–1978.

Provenance: Private collection, Germany.

The central relief panel, depicting the Adoration of the Shepherds, is modelled after a drawing by Hans Rottenhammer (1564–1625) in the Germanisches Nationalmuseum, Nuremberg.

H. G. KLEIN, COLOGNE

TAZZA

Dutch, 1601.

Dated on the tablet at immediate left of pedestal (AD/DCI), with initials WMG below that. On left tablet are the letters DE/GDH/IT. Also, mark for native Dutch works.

Silver, gilt, cast, chased, and engraved; 5½" H, 7" diam. (14.5, 17.5 cm).

Literature: *Katalog Frederik Muller*, Amsterdam, 1911, p. 9, ill. no. 308; J. W. Frederiks, *Dutch Silver*, The Hague, 1952, p. 55, ill. no. 33.

Exhibition: Niederrheinisches Frei-lichtmuseum, Grefrath, 1977.

Provenance: Private collection, The Netherlands.

Represented in relief are Charity and two children seated on an altar, surrounded by Faith at left and Hope at right. Two angels hold a wreath overhead.

H. G. KLEIN, COLOGNE

GALLON DRY MEASURE

English, 1601, Elizabeth I.

Inscribed: ELIZABETH REGINA 1601 (with crest and initials ER).

Cast-bronze; 10″ H, 7½″ top diam., 6″ base diam. (25.5, 19, 15 cm).

Exhibition: City of Bristol Museum and Art Gallery, 1979.

Provenance: B. Isher, Cheltenham.

ARTHUR BRETT AND SONS, NORWICH.

into the British Isles—it is important to remember that the primacy in value placed on pictures today did not exist in the seventeenth century. At the sale of the collection of Charles I, for example, his horse trappings, bridle, saddle, and other tack were sold as a lot and brought the same price as his most famous painting, Raphael's *La Perla*, then considered a masterpiece. (In 1604, the Gonzagas had given 50,000 scudi, the price of a princely palazzo, for this painting!) Even more startling, a stool covered in brown velvet equaled one-fourth the price of Titian's *Doge Andrea Gritti*, now one of the supreme masterpieces in the National Gallery in Washington, D.C. Imagine four stools being as costly as one of the world's greatest portraits!

Even in the field of painting there were anomalies. Although Charles's taste was catholic in scope and caused him to buy works by Dürer and Holbein, he had certain blind spots. He undervalued Rembrandt, for example. His collection contained only three canvases by the greatest Dutch master, and when they were sold none of them fetched more than five pounds. The king spent his money elsewhere, buying the finest Italian paintings of the sixteenth century, those of Annibale Carracci and Caravaggio, and seventeenth-century works by Rubens and Van Dyck.

Both Rubens and Van Dyck worked for Charles I, and both died rich men. Rubens was particularly wealthy, skillfully managing the torrential production of his paintings factory. He was a shrewd businessman, as revealed by his dealings with Sir Dudley Carleton, the British representative at The Hague and Charles I's art agent there. The correspondence between artist and ambassador reveals that Rubens painted many pictures for stock. When Sir Dudley, recently arrived from a diplomatic post in Venice, wanted some of the artist's work, he was offered twelve pictures valued at 8,850 florins; Rubens provided a list describing how much of each

painting he had done himself. Meanwhile, the painter had cast a covetous eye on the ambassador's own classical collection, mostly acquired in Venice, which was valued at 6,000 florins. After negotiations, Rubens exchanged nine of the pictures on his list, which he valued at 4,000 florins, for all the classical art he wanted. There remained 2,000 florins worth of Sir Dudley's collection which Sir Dudley gave Rubens in exchange for tapestries. A few years later, Rubens sold the bulk of his collection of marbles to the Duke of Buckingham at a good profit; and when the Duke of Buckingham was assassinated shortly thereafter, his widow sent these statues and busts back to Antwerp to be auctioned. This gave Rubens the opportunity to purchase what he wanted, making the whole deal eminently satisfactory to him.

At the time the collection of Charles I was being sold, another great collector, Cardinal Mazarin, was living in exile in Cologne. The works of art he had amassed in Paris stagger the imagination and rank only a little below Charles's. The French Parliament, knowing that the cardinal could always be bribed with a great painting or piece of sculpture, ordered his collection confiscated and auctioned. The young Louis XIV annulled the decree. The commissioners, appointed by Parliament, defied the king and announced the sale anyway. How far it actually went is unknown. But in 1652, after two years of exile, Mazarin returned to Paris, was welcomed by the king, resumed his former splendor, and continued his collecting. Mazarin's passion for art is portrayed in this touching scene described by the Duc de Brienne:

I was strolling through the new rooms [of the Mazarin palace in Paris]. I was in the little gallery where there was the [suite of tapestries] on the theme of Scipio. The Cardinal had none more beautiful. I heard [the Cardinal] com-

CONTINUED ON PAGE 49

45

LONG TABLE ▲

Chinese, late sixteenth–early seventeenth century, Ming Dynasty.

Black lacquer with crushed abalone shell (*laque burgautée*); 34 × 72½ × 23" (86 × 184 × 58 cm).

GARRICK C. STEPHENSON, NEW YORK

PAIR OF TALL CABINETS ▶

Chinese, Ming Dynasty, c. 1600 A.D.

Black lacquer, wood, mother-of-pearl; 69 × 35¾ × 22¼" (175 × 91 × 56 cm).

GARRICK C. STEPHENSON, NEW YORK

STONE CARVING

Flemish, second half of the seventeenth century, Baroque.

Carved turquoise, silver frame; 5¼ × 7⅛ × ½″ (13.5 × 18 × 1.5 cm).

Marked with a monogram of "VH" or "IVH".

Exhibited: Antiques Dealers' Fair, Delft, 1980.

The subject depicted is the wedding of Poseidon and Thetis.

JOSEPH M. MORPURGO, AMSTERDAM

ing by the noise of his slippers, in which he was shuffling along as a man does who is still greatly weakened by serious illness. I hid behind the tapestry, and I heard him exclaiming, "I must leave all this!" At each step he would halt, for he had no strength, he would glance this way or that, studying this object or that, and from the heart itself, he would cry out: "I must leave all this!" And turning again, he would add: "And that, too! How much trouble I've taken to collect all these things! How can I say farewell to them without sadness? . . . [Yet] I shall not see them again where I am going!" I could not contain a heavy sigh, and he heard me. "Who's there?" he said. "Who's there?" "It is I, Monseigneur," [I answered] . . . . "Come near, come near," he said in a very weak voice. He was naked in his woolen dressing gown trimmed with gray fur, and he was wearing his nightcap. He said to me, "Give me your hand, I'm very weak, I can't go on for very long . . . ." And going back to his former thought: "Look well, old friend, at that beautiful Correggio, and that Titian Venus, and that incomparable Deluge by Annibale Carracci; for I know you like pictures and understand them. Ah! my poor friend, I must leave all this! Good-bye, dear pictures which I have so much loved, which have cost me so dear!"

This heartrending vignette must touch any collector faced with an ultimate farewell to beloved treasures. (I have used a translation of the above by Joseph Alsop, published in his brilliant book, *The Rare Art Traditions*, to which I owe so much of this introduction.)

In Holland, as in England and France, collecting flourished in the seventeenth century. Many Dutch painters were dealers who constantly dabbled in the art market. Of these, two of the most famous were Rembrandt and Vermeer. Rembrandt frequently went to auctions, where he seems to have suffered from auction-fever, usually overbidding for anything he wanted. This disease contributed to his ultimate bankruptcy, and when he could no longer pay his creditors, including the owner of his house, his possessions were put up for sale. The auction took place at the Imperial Crown, the inn where he moved when he was forced to leave his home. The first auction was a dismal failure. A second was held in late 1658 and realized the ludicrously low sum of 5,000 florins. Two art dealers, Lodewyck van Ludik and Adrian de Wees, testified that Rembrandt had spent 11,600 florins on his collection, exclusive of paintings, between 1640 and 1650. For paintings he must have spent as much again, given his uncontrollable passion to outbid all competitors. Little wonder that his son Titus was appointed his financial custodian.

Vermeer, unlike Rembrandt, was a dealer rather than a collector. Most of his income must have come from art sales, since he was reluctant to part with his own pictures, which he painted so slowly. Vermeer was also considered an expert in Old Masters, and in this capacity he frequently gave advice. In one instance, the prominent Amsterdam dealer Gerritt Uylenburgh, Rembrandt's brother-in-law, sold thirteen pictures for 30,000 guilders to the Elector of Brandenberg. The sale included paintings attributed to the most famous artists: Michelangelo, Giorgione, Raphael, Titian, and Holbein, among others. Suspicion about authenticity was aroused, so the elector consulted various experts in Amsterdam. Some considered the pictures poor; others said they were not so bad. The elector was bewildered by these conflicting responses and arranged for the canvases to be brought to The Hague. Vermeer was sent for in the hope of receiving a more definite opinion. His judgment has been preserved, and in giving it he used no

CONTINUED ON PAGE 75

HENDRIK VAN BALEN (1575–1632) AND JAN BRUEGHEL II (1601–1678)▲

Sine Cerere et Baccho Friget Venus

Flemish, 1625.

Signed, on pedestal: H.V.BALEN. With indistinct date lower right and illegible signature of Brueghel.

Oil on panel, 24½ × 38" (62 × 96 cm).

Literature: To be included in *Oeuvre-verzeichnis und Tagebuch des Jan Brueghel II*, being prepared by Dr. Klaus Ertz.

Provenance: Backofen-Burckart, Basel, 1824–1976.

GALERIE MÜLLENMEISTER, SOLINGEN

NICOLAES KNÜPFER (1603–1660)▶

Wine Is the Milk of Venus

German, c. 1640.

Oil on panel; 19½ × 23½" (49 × 60 cm).

Literature: Friedrich Schlie, *Über Nicolaes Knüpfer und Einige Seiner Gemälde*, Schwerin, 1896, ill. no. 12.

Provenance: J. de Kuyper, Rotterdam (as *Wine, Woman, and Song*).

GALERIE MÜLLENMEISTER, SOLINGEN

51

ABRAHAM BLOEMAERT (1564–1651)

The Judgment of Paris

Dutch, 1636.

Signed and dated, lower right.

Oil on canvas, 36½ × 48″ (92.8 × 122 cm).

**H. SHICKMAN GALLERY,
NEW YORK**

LUCA FERRARI, known as LUCA DA REGGIO (1605–1654)

Jupiter, Mercury, and Virtue

Italian, 1640.

Oil on canvas; 51 × 66½″ (130 × 169 cm).

Literature: J. von Schlosser, *Jahrbuch der Preussischen Kunstsammlungen*, 1900, vol. XXI, p. 262 ff.; M. Degani, *Mostra di Luca da Reggio*, Reggio Emilia, 1954, p. 22; A. Pallucchini, ed., in M. Boschini, *La Carta del Navegar Pitoresco*, Venice-Rome, 1966, p. 602, note 26; F. Gibbons, *Dosso and Battista Dossi*, Princeton, 1968, p. 213.

Provenance: Francesco and Giuseppe Bonfadini, Venice, before 1660 (as *Jove Painting the Wings of Butterflies and Mercury Keeping Virtue Away*); G. Scharnowski, Munich.

For a long time, this painting had been declared lost.

GALERIE BRUNO MEISSNER, ZÜRICH

FRANS SNYDERS (1579–1657)

Still Life with Fruit and Game

Flemish, first half of the seventeenth century.

Signed, at lower right: F. SNYDERS. FECIT.

Oil on canvas; 36 × 54" (91 × 137 cm).

Provenance: Baron Freiherr G. von Polnitz, Castle Aschbach, near Bamberg.

H. SHICKMAN GALLERY, NEW YORK

GEORG FLEGEL (1563–1638)

Still Life

German, c. 1630.

Oil on canvas; 24½ × 18¼″ (62.2 × 46.4 cm).

Exhibition: "Stilleben in Europa," Westfälisches Landesmuseum, Münster, and Staatliche Kunsthalle, Baden-Baden, November 1979– June 1980, cat. no. 222, ill. p. 423.

RICHARD GREEN (FINE PAINTINGS), LONDON

GIOVANNI BENEDETTO CASTIGLIONE (1609–1663/1665)

Abraham's Departure for the Land of Canaan

Italian, c. 1645–1650.

Inscribed, upper right: GENES XII.

Oil on canvas; 55½ × 91″ (141 × 231 cm).

Literature: Dr. Waagen, *Galleries and Cabinets of Art in Great Britain* (supplementary vol. to *The Treasures of Art in Great Britain*), London, 1857, p. 333 (as *The Departure of the Israelites from Egypt*); George Scharf, *A Descriptive and Historical Catalogue of the Collection of Pictures at Woburn Abbey*, London, 1890, pp. 228–229, no. 361 (as *Departure of the Israelites out of Egypt*); Horace Walpole, *Visits to Country Seats, etc.*, Oxford, 1927–1928, vol. X, p. 17 (as *Jacob Leaving Laban*).

Provenance: Sir Robert Walpole, before 1736 (as *Jacob Returning to Canaan*, no. 3 in manuscript inventory of his collection, dated 1736); Anonymous sale, London, 1748; Duke of Bedford, Woburn Abbey, Bedfordshire.

PAUL ROSENBERG & CO. INC., NEW YORK

JAN VAN KESSEL I (1626–1679)

Vanitas

Flemish, 1644.

Signed and dated, lower left: J.V. KESSEL. FECIT ANNO 1644.

Oil on canvas; 42⅛ × 33⅛″ (107 × 84 cm).

Provenance: The Van den Brök Collection.

Van Kessel painted the still life, while the figures, representing Death coming to take away Beauty, were probably painted by Jan Van Balen (1611–1654).

DIDIER AARON, INC., NEW YORK

57

GIOVANNI FRANCESCO BARBIERI, known as IL GUERCINO (1591–1666)

Study for the Figure of Ahasuerus

Italian, c. 1639.

Inscribed, at lower left: GUERCINO.

Pen and sepia ink with wash; 9¼ × 7″ (23.5 × 17.8 cm).

Provenance: Barberini collection; Private collection, Europe.

The figure in profile is a study for Ahasuerus in the painting *Esther before Ahasuerus*, in the University of Michigan Museum of Art, Ann Arbor; there is also a preliminary drawing for the painting in that museum's collection. According to the authority Denis Mahon, Guercino's records, which are extant, indicate that the drawing was paid for in 1639.

SPENCER A. SAMUELS & COMPANY, LTD., NEW YORK

REMBRANDT HARMENSZ VAN RIJN (1606–1669)

Woman in Profile

Dutch, c. 1634

Pen and brown ink, 3¾ × 2½″
(9.4 × 6 cm).

Literature: Otto Benesch, *The Drawings of Rembrandt*, London, 1973,
vol. II, no. 251, fig. 278.

Provenance: Robert Udney, England;
Richard Cosway; The Earl of War-
wick, 1936; W. Mertens, Leipzig.

**S. NIJSTAD OUDE KUNST B.V.,
THE HAGUE**

REMBRANDT HARMENSZ VAN RIJN (1606–1669)

The Three Crosses

Dutch, begun 1653, reworked c. 1660.

Publisher's inscription, at bottom center: FRANS CARELSE EXCUDIT.

Etching, drypoint, and engraving; on paper; fifth state of five; watermark: Strasburg Lily; 15⅛ × 17¾" (38.5 × 45.3 cm).

Literature: Adam Bartsch, *Catalogue raisonné de toutes les estampes qui forment l'oeuvre de Rembrandt et ceux de ses principaux imitateurs*, "Composé par Gersaint, Helle, Glomy et Yver. Nouvelle édition entièrement refondue, corrigée et considérablement augmentée," Vienna, 1797, no. 78; Arthur M. Hind, *A Catalogue of Rembrandt's Etchings Chronologically Arranged and Completely Illustrated*, 2 vols., 2nd ed., London, 1923, no. 270; *Hollstein's Dutch and Flemish Etchings, Engravings, and Woodcuts*, vol. XVIII, compiled by Christopher White and K. G. Boon, Amsterdam, 1969, no. 78.

Provenance: A. C. Poggi (until first quarter of the nineteenth century), Lugt 617; A. Firmin-Didot (1790–1870), Lugt 119; J. J. Peoli (1825–1893), Lugt 2020; A. J. Godby (1853–1934), Lugt 1119B; G. W. Nowell-Usticke; Private collection, United States.

DAVID TUNICK, INC., NEW YORK

JACOB JORDAENS (1593–1678)

The Road to Calvary

Flemish, c. 1655.

Oil on canvas; 94 × 68¾″ (239 × 174.5 cm).

Literature: Erik Burg Berger, "An Unknown Work by Jacob Jordaens," *The Burlington Magazine*, LXVIII, March 1936, pp. 139–140, ill.; Agnes Mongan, "A Jordaens Drawing," *The Burlington Magazine*, LXXV, December 1939, pp. 245–246, ill.; Agnes Mongan and Paul J. Sachs, *Drawings in the Fogg Museum of Art*, Cambridge, Mass., 1940, under no. 480, fig. 247; Leo van Puyvelde, *Jordaens*, Paris and Brussels, 1953, pp. 147, 192; Roger A. d'Hulst, *De Tekeningen van Jakob Jordaens*, Brussels, 1956, pp. 294, 398; Michael Jaffé, *Jacob Jordaens 1593–1678*, Ottawa, 1968, no. 111, p. 137 in cat.

Exhibitions: "Zes Eeuwen Katholiek," Amsterdam (Waag), June-July 1946, no. 71; "Jacob Jordaens," The National Gallery of Canada, 1968, no. 111.

Provenance: The Dutch province of the Society of Jesus, The Hague, but placed in the Church of St. Francis Xavier (De Krijtberg), Amsterdam, sometime after 1654.

NOORTMAN & BROD, LTD., LONDON

◄ OVERMANTEL MIRROR AND PAINTING

Mirror: English, early eighteenth century, Queen Anne.

Painting: *Patriarchal Journey*, attributed to Johann Heinrich Roos (1631–1685), c. 1650.

Bevelled glass; oil on canvas; 71½ × 66″ (181.5 × 167.5 cm).

Roos came to Rome from the Palatine in 1650 and for the next six years absorbed the classical Baroque tradition. On his return to Germany, he became Court Painter to Karl-Ludwig of the Palatine.

VERNAY & JUSSEL, INC., NEW YORK

CABINET ON STAND ▲

German, c. 1650, Baroque.

Exterior of walnut veneer, interior of natural and stained European woods, including beech, ash, and fruitwoods; pine carcase; mother-of-pearl, steel; 51½ × 40 × 18½″ (129 × 101 × 47 cm).

Similar example: Rijksmuseum, Amsterdam (see *Mobili Tedeschi*, Milan, 1969, pp. 22–23).

DALVA BROTHERS, INC., NEW YORK

FLAGELLATION GROUP

Italian (Rome), mid-seventeenth century, Baroque.

Based upon a model by Alessandro Algardi (d. 1654); possibly after a design by the Flemish artist Duquesnoy.

Gilt-bronze; 10″ H (25.5 cm).

Similar examples: Martin D'Arcy Gallery of Art, The Loyola University Museum of Medieval and Renaissance Art, Chicago (see *The First Ten Years*, catalogue of the Martin D'Arcy Gallery of Art, 1979, no. 78, ill.); Kunsthistorisches Museum, Vienna.

Provenance: Private collection, Europe.

SPENCER A. SAMUELS & COMPANY, LTD., NEW YORK

PAIR OF HORSES

Italian (Venice), early seventeenth century.

Bronze, gilt-bronze; 8⁷⁄₈″ H (22.5 cm).

Literature: Rosenberg & Stiebel, Inc., New York, *European Works of Art III*, 1981, pp. 52–53.

ROSENBERG & STIEBEL, INC., NEW YORK

DAVID TENIERS II (1610–1690) AND JAN VAN KESSEL I (1626–1679)

Conquest of a Town by Count Moncada

Flemish, 1664.

Signed in two places: at right center, D. TENIERS; at lower right, J.V. KESSEL F.

Oil on copper; 21¼ × 27″ (54 × 69 cm).

Literature: To be included in a forthcoming book on David Teniers by Dr. M. Klinge.

Provenance: Marquis de Villafranca; F. Kleinberger, Paris, 1925; W. H. Corbitt, Paris.

Two companion pieces to this painting are in the Thyssen-Bornemisza Collection in Lugano, Switzerland.

KUNSTHANDEL XAVER SCHEIDWIMMER, MUNICH

**OTTO MARSEUS VAN SCHRIECK
(1619–1678)**

Flowers in a Glass Vase with Lizard

Dutch, 1661.

Signed and dated, lower right: OTTO
MARSEUS 1661.

Oil on canvas; 23¼ × 19″ (59 × 48 cm).

Literature: Peter Mitchell, *European
Flower Painters*, London, 1973, p.
28, ill. no. 28.

Provenance: Jack Linsky, New York.

**KUNSTHANDEL XAVER
SCHEIDWIMMER, MUNICH**

◄ **PALACE VASE**

Chinese, Ch'ing Dynasty, K'ang Hsi period, 1662–1722 A.D.

Famille verte porcelain; 29½″ H (75 cm).

Literature: *Catalogue of the Chinese Porcelain in the Collection of J. Pierpont Morgan*, vol. II, no. 1200. Ill. pl. no. XCV, case S, described on p. 59.

Exhibited: The Metropolitan Museum of Art, New York (in the J. Pierpont Morgan collection for more than twenty-five years).

Provenance: Marsden J. Perry; J. Pierpont Morgan; Duveen Brothers, New York.

RALPH M. CHAIT GALLERIES, INC., NEW YORK

FIGURE OF KUEI HSIEN, THE STAR GOD OF LETTERS ►

Chinese, Ch'ing Dynasty, K'ang Hsi period, 1662–1722 A.D.

Three-color glazed biscuit porcelain; 9⅞″ H (25 cm).

Literature: Edgar Gorer and J. F. Blacker, *Chinese Porcelain and Hard Stones*, London, 1911, vol. I, pl. 79.

Provenance: Mrs. Hans Scherr-Thoss.

RALPH M. CHAIT GALLERIES, INC., NEW YORK

SET OF TWELVE APOSTLE SPOONS

English (London), 1637, Charles I.

Richard Crosse, silversmith.

Hallmarks for London 1637. Marked RC with three pellets above and a quatrefoil and two pellets below.

Inscribed: W.I.H. 1637; nimbus of each chased with the Saint Esprit.

Silver; 7 to 7½″ H (18 to 19 cm).

Literature: Charles G. Rupert, *Apostle Spoons*, London, 1929, p. 10, pl. XXI.

Provenance: Rev. B. P. Symons, D.D., of Wadham College, Oxford; Canon Valpy.

The figures represented are: The Master holding an orb and cross, His right hand upheld in blessing; St. Bartholomew, with a butcher's knife; St. Jude, with a carpenter's square; St. Philip, with a long staff and a cross in the T; St. Thomas, with a spear; St. Andrew, with a saltire cross; St. James the Less, with a fuller's bat; St. Peter, with a key; St. James the Greater, with a pilgrim's staff; St. John, with the cup of sorrow; St. Matthias, with a halberd; and St. Simon Zelotes, with a long saw.

S. J. SHRUBSOLE, LTD., LONDON

PAIR OF CHINOISERIE SALVERS

English (London), 1683, Charles II.

Both hallmarked for London, 1683. On top of plate, both marked WF with bow knot above, rosette below. On back of both plates are two crests, one with the words *Dieu et ma patrie*, the

other with *Honi soit qui mal y pense*.

Silver; one, 2⅝ × 8¾ × 8¾″ (6.5 × 22 × 22 cm); other, 2⅝ × 8⅞ × 8⅞″ (6.5 × 22.5 × 22.5 cm).

Exhibited: Wadsworth Atheneum,

Hartford; Art Institute of Chicago; Sterling and Francine Clark Art Institute, Williamstown, Massachusetts.

S. J. PHILLIPS LTD., LONDON

KOVSH

Russian, c. 1684.

Silver, silver-gilt, cast, chased, and engraved; 12″ L (31 cm); weight: 397 gr.

On the inside of the bowl are engraved the two-headed eagle of the tsar and a laurel wreath. The circular inscription in Russian, translated, reads that on December 4, 1684, this kovsh was presented by the two reigning tsars, Ivan V and Peter I, to Ivan Semjonov, ataman of the Don cossacks, for his faithful service.

Literature: Leon Grinberg, *Metal Work and Enamels*; Catalogue of Russian Art, London, 1935; M. M. Postnikowa-Losewa, *Russian Silver and Gold Kovshes* (in Russian), Moscow, vol. X, 1953.

Exhibitions: Russian Art Exhibition, London, 1935; West German Art Fair, Düsseldorf, 1982.

MEINZ-ARNOLD, HAMBURG

ICON

Our Lady of Vladimir

Russian (Moscow), seventeenth century.

Wood, gold, niello, rubies, diamonds, emeralds, seed pearls, enamel; $12\frac{1}{4} \times 10\frac{5}{8}''$ (31 × 27 cm).

Exhibited: "Exhibition of Russian Art," London (1 Belgrave Square), 1935; Baltimore Museum of Art, 1942; Worcester Art Museum, 1942; Phoenix Fine Art Association, 1961; "Russian Icons," A La Vieille Russie, New York, 1962, cat. no. 55; "Symbols of Faith," Explorers Hall, National Geographic Society, Washington, D.C., 1982.

Provenance: The family of Count Tolstoy.

Russian gold artifacts of the period before Peter the Great, such as this icon, are extremely rare, since most were either destroyed or melted down to mint coins.

A LA VIEILLE RUSSIE, INC., NEW YORK

STATE ARMCHAIR

English, last decade of the seventeenth century, William & Mary.

Walnut; 52¼ × 27 × 20½″ (132.5 × 68.5 × 52 cm).

Similar examples: Victoria and Albert Museum, London (pair) See H. H. Mulliner, *The Decorative Arts in England, 1660–1780*, London, 1923, ch. 1, fig. 6; P. Macquoid and R. Edwards, *The Dictionary of English Furniture*, London, 1954, p. 248, ill.

The design of this chair is very much in the manner of Daniel Marot, architect and designer to William III.

M. DARLING LIMITED, NEW YORK

weasel words: "They are so poor that they do not deserve the name of any good artist, let alone the exalted names they have."

Toward the end of Vermeer's life, the art market fell on very bad times. This was even true in Amsterdam, the principal center of trade. Circumstances could hardly have been less favorable: there was war between France and Holland, the Commonwealth had ruined the aristocracy in England, and none of the other countries at that time were important sources of patronage. After its dikes were opened in 1672 to prevent a French invasion, Holland suffered terrible inflation, rising taxes, and drastic curtailment of all luxury purchases. Vermeer was forced to liquidate his stock of Old Masters, move into a small house, and borrow money. When he died in 1675, his widow was crushed by heavy debts, and she applied for bankruptcy, saying her husband had been unable to sell anything because of the war. This severe depression in the art market lasted until the eighteenth century.

**THOMAS GAINSBOROUGH
(1727–1788)**

A Wooded River Landscape

English, c.1756.

Oil on canvas; 29 × 44″ (73.5 × 112 cm).

Literature: To be included in the forthcoming catalogue of Gainsborough's paintings by Dr. John Hayes.

Provenance: Lady Eaton.

RICHARD GREEN (FINE PAINTINGS), LONDON

EIGHTEENTH CENTURY

In France, the eighteenth century opened with an economic disaster known as John Law's Bubble, named for a Scottish banker; an orgy of speculation that he encouraged virtually ruined the entire court. To avoid bankruptcy, nobles were forced to sell their collections abroad; and when they again became collectors, under the leadership of Mme de Pompadour, they sought the work of their contemporaries, not of the old-fashioned masters. The situation was somewhat similar to the one in America today, where private picture collections are limited primarily to paintings from Impressionism onward. It is difficult to think of Boucher and Fragonard as the eighteenth-century equivalents of Jackson Pollock and Andy Warhol, but that is what they were.

Mme de Pompadour established the tastes of the day. She and her brother, the Marquis de Marigny, appointed Boucher to succeed Coypel as *Premier Peintre du Roi*, and these three became the arbiters of fashion. Around 1740 a mania for soft-paste porcelain developed. Mme de Pompadour took over a pavilion at Sèvres for its manufacture, working in the factory herself as a designer and artisan. When unglazed biscuit was developed by Bachelier, she encouraged its use and presented French sculptors with a new, marketable medium. This passion for porcelain at the French court was increased by an economic factor: as the nobles found themselves in financial straits, they melted down their silver to pay their debts and adopted porcelain for their service. But as soon as prosperity was restored—or seemed to be—those who were rich enough gave up eating off china and resumed their practice of ordering services from goldsmiths. The best of these craftsmen, Germain, Caffieri, and others, designed new models for their aristocratic clients.

With the return of better times, new collectors appeared. Collecting drawings and prints became popular, for they were less expensive than paintings or sculpture. Pierre Crozat, for example, assembled an unrivaled collection of drawings. Before he died, he named a fellow collector, Mariette, as his executor and instructed him to prepare a catalogue for his estate sale, which realized 300,000 livres for charity. It is said that Mariette, who was a dealer as well, hid many of the best items and acquired them himself. Mariette died in 1774, and his will tendered his collection *en bloc* to the king for 100,000 livres, but the offer was refused. Later it was sold for 300,000 livres. A dealer at the sale, Lempereur, bidding on behalf of the Ministry of Fine Arts, bought as many fine drawings as the sum allotted to him, 120,000 livres, would permit. These are today among the greatest treasures of the Bibliothèque Nationale. But for 20,000 livres less, the entire collection might have become the property of the state.

Though the eighteenth century was a period when the French tended to sell art rather than acquire it, there were numerous dealers—among them Gersaint, who had great personal charm and was a fine connoisseur, two qualities of paramount importance for success in art dealing. The rich industrialist Jean de Julienne was among the collec-

CONTINUED ON PAGE 81

◄ **JEAN-BAPTISTE BLIN DE FONTENAY (1653–1715)**

Le Buffet sous la treille (*Buffet under a Trellis*)

French, c. 1700.

Signed, lower right: FONTENAY 170(0); the last number seems to have been touched up.

Oil on canvas; 90½ × 85¾" (228 × 216 cm).

Literature: Robert Rosenblum, "Reconstructing French Art," introduction to exhibition catalogue *Four Guest Galleries from Paris and Paul Rosenberg & Co.*, New York, 1982, pp. 4, 24.

Exhibition: "Four Guest Galleries from Paris and Paul Rosenberg & Co., French Painting 1600–1900," Paul Rosenberg & Co., New York, March–May 1982, no. 9, ill. p. 24.

This painting may have been shown at the 1704 Paris Salon.

CAILLEUX, PARIS

English (London), 1700, William III.

Thomas Jenkins, silversmith; hallmarks for London 1700.

Inscribed with arms of Daniell and motto *Nil sperno nec miror nec metuo*.

Silver; 11" H, 15" diam. (28, 38 cm); weight: 131 oz.

Literature: Georgina E. Lee, *British Silver Monteith Bowls*, London, 1978.

Provenance: Sir Frank H. Hollins.

JAMES ROBINSON INC., NEW YORK

HERMAN HENSTENBURGH (1667–1726) AND PIETER WITHOOS (1654–1693)

Dutch, 1700.

Collection of gouaches bound in leather and entitled *Drawings of Insects by Henstenburgh*, comprising twelve original gouaches on paper by Henstenburgh, one on vellum by Withoos. Bound c. 1790 in straight grain crimson morocco, the sides tooled to a gilt Greek key border, with gilt fillets and floral tools, gilt back.

Henstenburgh gouaches signed: HB FEC.

Volume: 15¼ × 12¾ × ¾″ (38.8 × 32.4 × 2 cm).

Each drawing: 8¾ × 11¼″ (22.3 × 28.8 cm).

Similar example: Auction catalogue, Max I. Friedländer-Ten Cate, Amsterdam, 1959, no. 178, pl. 16.

Provenance: Private collection, Canada.

The drawings represent butterflies, moths, beetles, and caterpillars and have been tipped onto sheets of Holland paper with pen and ink and wash borders.

LUCIEN GOLDSCHMIDT, INC., NEW YORK

Illustrated here: Single drawing by Henstenburgh.

tors who put themselves completely in Gersaint's hands. Gersaint was fortunate enough to have his signboard painted by Watteau. A Watteau painting shows the interior of Gersaint's shop filled with pictures, several of which are about to be packed. From seeing his signboard, one would never guess the miscellaneous stock on which he and his descendants, who were also dealers, had to depend for their profit. In this respect, an advertisement placed in the *Mercure de France* during the Revolution is revealing. As quoted by Maurice Rheims in *Art on the Market*, it reads:

> Sieur Gersaint, a dealer at the Pont Notre Dame, who has been travelling for many years collecting unique curios, has recently returned to Paris with a rare and wonderful assortment . . . pagodas and other porcelains from Japan, strange and attractive figures of all types from the Indies. Sieur Gersaint has just started a new business in wrought iron and other tasteful and useful goods, whose quality, function, design, and utility should satisfy the most astringent critics. He is in a position to suit private individuals and traders alike with hundreds of things at reasonable prices.

Picture dealing in itself evidently was not sufficiently profitable. We shall see this was true not only in France but also in England, for Colnaghi's, who started in Paris, and Agnew's, who began in Manchester, both commenced with similar miscellaneous items for sale in the eighteenth century. Shops had to be sufficiently large to accommodate such a varied stock, and further proof of the size of Gersaint's was its use as an auction house. Unfortunately, there are no records of sales, but first-class works of art from the important private collections probably were sold by private treaty and did not pass through the hands of the Gersaints.

In terms of the decorative arts, the *marchands-merciers* were tastemakers on the level of Mme de Pompadour. These powerful dealers offered gilt–bronze *objets*, lacquer, porcelain, furniture, and other types of furnishings to their wealthy clients. In fact, it was they who are said to have created the vogue for mounted Oriental porcelain, a *de rigueur* appointment in French interiors of the time. Great *ébénistes* often worked exclusively for these dealers-cum-decorators. One example was Bernard Van Risenburgh, the *ébéniste* to Lazare-Duvaux, who himself was an influential personage in the court of Louis XV.

The profits of art dealers in eighteenth-century France were modest. For example, Lazare-Duvaux's total business over a period of ten years, from 1748 to 1758, amounted to 2,845,000 old francs, or just over $5,000 (a sum whose real value is about $100,000 today). During these ten years, Mme de Pompadour alone spent 376,000 livres, of which 13,933 were for forty-nine commodes. Lazare-Duvaux's daybooks indicate that a large percentage of his sales represented Christmas shopping. After December, the next best months were April, May, and June, when foreigners would come to Paris and buy avidly.

A dealer of more exalted station than those mentioned so far was Jean-Baptiste-Pierre Le Brun, consort of that unhappily married and fashionable painter, Elizabeth Vigée, who managed to portray nearly everyone worth knowing except her husband. Le Brun and Vigée owned a large house in the Rue de Cléry, where they assembled a salon—one of the most brilliant of its time—and built a set of adjoining rooms where Le Brun kept his own collection and sold important Old Masters. On two occasions, in 1790 and 1792, he also showed contemporary paintings, for which he received a letter from Greuze conveying thanks on behalf of the artists of Paris, who were disenchanted with the Academy.

CONTINUED ON PAGE 85

81

◄ **TAPESTRY SCREEN**

French (Paris), c. 1715, Louis XIV.

Made at the Savonnerie Manufactory, probably designed by Jean-Baptiste Blin de Fontenay (1653–1715).

Dyed wool on linen warp and weft, wooden frame; each panel: 108 × 25″ (273 × 64 cm).

Literature: *Louis XIV, fastes et décors*, Louvre, Paris, 1960, ill. pl. CII.

Exhibitions: "Tapis de la Savonnerie," Manufacture des Gobelins, 1926–1927, no. 96; "Le Siècle de Louis XIV," Bibliothèque Nationale, 1927, no. 1268; "Louis XIV, Fastes et Décors," Louvre, Paris, 1960, no. 774.

Provenance: Mme d'Yvon, Paris (1892); Seligman, Paris.

DALVA BROTHERS, INC., NEW YORK

ARMCHAIR ►

English, c. 1720, George I.

Burr walnut; 39½ × 25½ × 23″ (100.5 × 65 × 58.5 cm).

G. RANDALL FINE ANTIQUES & WORKS OF ART, ALEXANDRIA

CARD TABLE

English, c. 1710, Queen Anne.

Burr walnut, parcel-gilt; with concertina action; 28 × 31¼ × 16″ (71 × 79.5 × 40.5 cm).

Provenance: Marjorie Wiggin Prescott Collection, Connecticut.

G. RANDALL FINE ANTIQUES & WORKS OF ART, ALEXANDRIA

It is amazing that a man closely associated with royalty (Le Brun was curator for both the Duc d'Orléans and the Comte d'Artois), should have survived the guillotine, particularly as his wife was touring the courts of Europe with a portrait of Marie Antoinette draped in black crepe. Le Brun even had the nerve to write an introduction to his commemorative sales catalogue, which appeared in 1792, that criticized "our politicians and moralists of the last few years who have been trying to diminish the reputation of Louis XIV." But he was not as brave as all that. The second volume, published a little later, opens thus: "This book, which was undertaken many years ago, was handed over to the printer before the glorious epoch which has turned an enslaved [people] into a free people. Begun under despotism, it is completed under the auspices of sacred equality and august freedom."

As Francis Haskell has pointed out:

The plan of his book was a new one, the artists being arranged neither alphabetically nor according to strict chronology, but in groups of pupils and followers around particular masters.... His whole book was designed to bring to light hitherto neglected artists such as Saenredam, and was specifically intended to replace name snobbery by what was in effect another kind of snobbery—that of the unknown—which was to open up infinite possibilities for historians and collectors.

Although Le Brun was one of the first art critics to attempt to reestablish forgotten painters, no one followed up his greatest discovery: the existence of Vermeer (who had been almost entirely forgotten) based on the detection of his signature on the Rothschild *Astronomer*. The reason, in part, for Vermeer's obscurity, as Haskell says, is simple. Collectors asked themselves, "Why buy an unrecognized painter like Vermeer when a famous artist like Metsu is available?" And perhaps Le Brun intended to remove the signature on the Rothschild picture and sell it as a Metsu. For the same reason, an interest in Quattrocento pictures may have been postponed when collectors put an identical question to themselves, "Who wants a Botticelli when a Guido Reni can be had for the asking?" It is when dealers run out of Guido Renis that they encourage a change of fashion and urge collectors to an appreciation of another period. Today it is Baroque painting; tomorrow it may be nineteenth-century Salon art.

At about this time, a remarkable event in the art market took place. Louis-Philippe-Joseph, head of a junior branch of the Orléans family, who was hoping to occupy the shaky throne of Louis XVI, sold his pictures to obtain money for his machinations. His collection at that time was probably the finest in the world, and he sold his Italian, French, and Northern pictures in England. A syndicate of three noblemen—the Duke of Bridgewater, Lord Stafford, and Lord Carlysle—bought all the Italian and French pictures and, after selling off what they did not want, realized a handsome profit. These were the greatest paintings to come to England since the days of Charles I.

The first proposal for acquiring the Italian masterpieces came from a dealer, a Mr. Bryan, who—to quote another dealer, Buchanan—"possessed the confidence of the Duke of Bridgewater," as necessary in this case as Knoedler's friendship with Andrew Mellon was for the acquisition of the Hermitage Gallery paintings. When the Orléans pictures arrived in England, they were displayed in two of Bryan's shops—one in Pall Mall, the other, called the Lyceum, in a less fashionable part of London. At the Lyceum, the pictures could be readily seen because the attendance there was sparse; as Miss Mary Berry wrote a friend in March 1799, "It is not near Dyde's and Scribe's, nor Butler's,

CONTINUED ON PAGE 89

PAIR OF ARM CHAIRS (FAUTEUILS À LA REINE)

French, c. 1774–1789, Louis XVI.

Jean Boucault (c. 1705–1786), *menuisier*.

Marked with the maker's mark and that of the Château of Versailles.

Gilt wood; 37½ × 28½ × 28½″ (95 × 72.5 × 72.5 cm).

DIDIER AARON, INC., NEW YORK

DOMENICO TIEPOLO (1727–1804)

The Coffin of Punchinello Unloaded from the Funeral Barque

Italian, c. 1797–1803.

Signed on plinth under bust at left: DOM TIEPOLO F.

Pen and golden-brown ink, brown wash over black chalk, on paper;

16 × 25¼″ (40.5 × 64 cm).

Literature: The Frick Collection, New York, *Domenico Tiepolo's Punchinello Drawings*, published by Indiana University Art Museum, 1979, No. S24, p. 147, ill. p. 123 (not in exhibition).

Exhibition: Musée des Arts Décoratifs, Paris, 1921.

Provenance: Anonymous sale, Sotheby, Wilkinson & Hodge, London, July 6, 1920; Colnaghi's, London; Richard Owen, Paris.

PAUL ROSENBERG & CO., NEW YORK

nor any of the great haberdashers for the women, nor Bond St., nor St. James's for the men." Even in the eighteenth century, the location of an art dealer's gallery was of the utmost importance!

With the confiscation of Louis XVI's property by the Revolutionary Tribunal, furniture and *objets d'art* of the highest quality were dispersed all over the Continent and also poured into England. The Versailles sale, which lasted for a whole year—from ten in the morning to eight at night—offered *antiquaires* opportunities never to occur again. As in the case of the property of Charles I, prices were ludicrously low. Although European royalty abstained from purchasing the possessions of the decapitated king, others had no such scruples. Dealers filled their warehouses with the finest porcelain, furniture, and silver made by the superb craftsmen of the eighteenth century. In fact, the great *ébéniste* Jean-Henri Riesener took advantage of the ridiculous prices to buy back the furniture he himself had made.

CONTINUED ON PAGE 149

TAPESTRY

Flemish, 1698–1738, probably 1733.

Guillaume Werniers (worked at Lille between 1720 and 1738)

Signed, bottom right: G. WERNIERS.

Wool, silk; 146 × 170" (370 × 430 cm).

Exhibtion: Antique Dealers' Fair, Delft, 1969.

Provenance: Prince von Schwartzenberg.

The design is after a painting by David Teniers the Younger.

PETERS' OUDE KUNST B.V., TILBURG

PLAQUE OF QUEEN ANNE

English (Lambeth), 1704.

Dated on reverse.

Blue and white delftware pottery;
9⅛ × 7¾″ (23 × 19.5 cm).

This portrait is probably after a
contemporary painting.

**PRICE GLOVER, INC.,
NEW YORK**

CENTERPIECE

Strasbourg, c. 1713, Baroque.

Joh. Michel Hibmaier, silversmith.

Ivory (elephant and narwhal tusk), silver-gilt; 12″ H (31 cm).

Hibmaier is mentioned in Hans Haug, *L'Orfèvrerie de Strasbourg dans les collection publiques françaises*, Paris, 1978, table III.

This spice holder comprises several parts: the base and cup, of narwhal tusk, are carved with fantastic sea creatures; the foot shows the embracing figures of Poseidon and Amphitrite; and at the top is a kneeling nymph, with a dolphin around her shoulders; both foot and top are of elephant tusk.

NEUSE-ANTIQUITÄTEN, BREMEN

TANKARD

German (Meissen), c. 1720

Böttger porcelain, silver-gilt; 6½"H, 4"diam. (15, 9.6 cm).

Marked at bottom with two crossed swords in underglaze blue; mounts (lid and ring at base) marked HKZ in triangular shield, with year, letter J and mark indicating made in Dresden, 1731–1737.

Decorated c. 1725 with Böttger luster and gold by Johann Ehrenfried Stadler; painted on it are a Chinese palace with flag and multicolored "Indianische Blumen."

GERHARD RÖBBIG, MUNICH

CENSER IN THE FORM OF A PAGODA FIGURE

German (Meissen), c. 1720.

Böttger porcelain; 4½″ H (11 cm).

Decorated with "Indianische Blumen" and gilt in the manner of Johann Schmischek.

Similar examples: See E. Zimmermann, *Erfindung und Frühzeit des Meissner Porzellans*, Berlin, 1908, p. 236, fig. 99; *Guide to the Collection of Early Meissen Porcelain, The C.I. and R.H. Wark Collection in the Cummer Gallery of Art*, Jacksonville, Florida, pp. 12–13, no. 12.

Meissen porcelain made from 1710 to about 1720 is referred to as "Böttger porcelain," after Johann Friedrich Böttger (1682–1719), the director of the factory from its founding in 1710 until his death.

GERHARD RÖBBIG, MUNICH

BUREAU-BOOKCASE

English, early eighteenth century, Queen Anne.

Black japanning, with gold chinoiserie; 64½ × 21½ × 14¾″ (164 × 54.5 × 37.5 cm).

Literature: Geoffrey Wills, *English Furniture 1550–1760*, Enfield, Middlesex, 1971, p. 118, fig. 92.

Similar example: See Ralph Edwards, *The Shorter Dictionary of English Furniture*, London, 1964, p. 76, pl. 14.

Provenance: Marjorie Wiggin Prescott Collection, Connecticut.

G. RANDALL FINE ANTIQUES & WORKS OF ART, ALEXANDRIA

TABLE

French, c. 1720, Régence.

Beechwood with Chinese lacquer top;
27½ × 34¾ × 22¼″ (70 × 88 ×
57 cm).

Literature: Guillaume Janneau,
    Le meuble léger en France, Paris, 1952,
    pl. 37.

Provenance: Louis Guiraud.

**GARRICK C. STEPHENSON,
NEW YORK**

BUREAU-BOOKCASE

English, c. 1710, Queen Anne.

Walnut; 91 × 43 × 23″ (231 × 109 × 58.5 cm).

PHILIP COLLECK OF LONDON LTD., NEW YORK

BUREAU-BOOKCASE

English, c. 1725–1740, George I, attributed to Giles Grendey (1693–1780).

Burr walnut, parcel-gilt, bevelled mirror, with original locks, handles, keys; 95 × 40 × 23″ (241.5 × 101.5 × 58.5 cm).

G. RANDALL FINE ANTIQUES & WORKS OF ART, ALEXANDRIA

▲ SIDE TABLE

English, c. 1730–1740, George II.

Wood, marble; 32 × 54 × 33″ (81.5 × 137 × 84 cm).

PRICE GLOVER, INC., NEW YORK

◄ PAIR OF SIDE CHAIRS

English, c. 1725, George I.

Walnut; 41¼ × 22 × 20″ (105 × 56 × 51 cm).

G. RANDALL FINE ANTIQUES & WORKS OF ART, ALEXANDRIA

ALEXANDRE-FRANÇOIS DESPORTES (1661–1743)

Still Life with Flowers, Fruit, Silver, and Game

French, 1736.

Signed and dated, at lower left: DESPORTES 1736.

Oil on canvas; 36 × 29″ (91 × 73 cm).

Literature: Salon Livret, 1737; M. & F. Faré, *La vie silencieuse en France, la nature morte au XVIIIe siècle*, Fribourg, 1976, p. 86, fig. 130.

Exhibition: Paris Salon, 1737.

Provenance: Montabeau Collection, Paris (sale, Paris, July 19, 1802, no. 27); Private collection, France.

MAURICE SEGOURA GALLERY, PARIS

JOHN WOOTTON (1686–1765)

Three King Charles Spaniels Beside a Classical Urn

English, c. 1730.

Signed at right: J. WOOTTON.

Oil on canvas; 57 × 47" (144.8 × 119.4 cm).

Literature: Arthur Ackermann & Son Ltd., London, *Ackermann's Annual Exhibition Catalogue*, October 1980, ill. no. 18.

Provenance: Rt. Rev. Spencer Madan, D.D., Bishop of Peterborough, 1813; Rev. Spencer Madan, 1873; C. Cressley; Col. R. Vallance.

ARTHUR ACKERMANN & SON LTD., LONDON

FIGURE OF A HOUND

Chinese, for the Western market, Ch'ing Dynasty, Ch'ien Lung period, 1736–1795 A.D.

Porcelain; 21¼ × 12⅞″ (54 × 32.5 cm).

Exhibition: "The Magnificent Menagerie," University Hospital Antiques Show, Philadelphia, 1978, cat. no. 35.

FRED B. NADLER ANTIQUES, INC., BAY HEAD

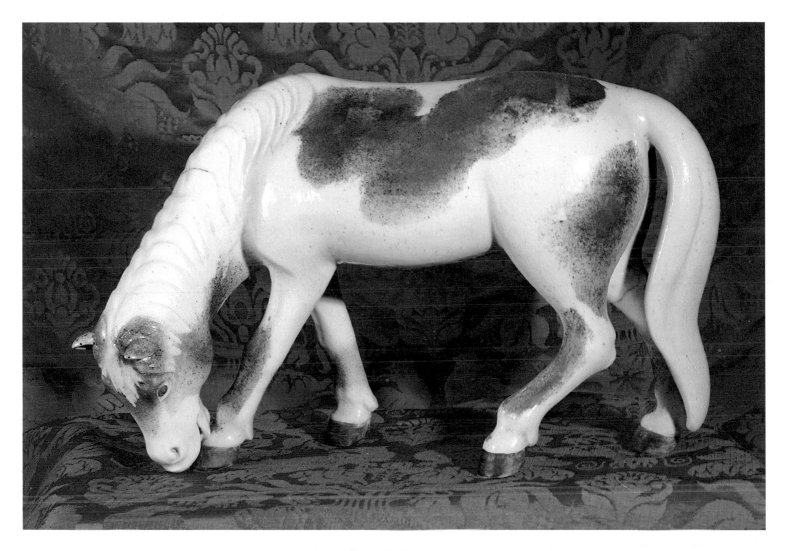

FIGURE OF A HORSE

Chinese, for the Western market,
Ch'ing Dynasty, Ch'ien Lung period,
1736–1795 A.D.

Porcelain; 11 × 17½″ (28 × 44.5 cm).

**FRED B. NADLER ANTIQUES,
INC., BAY HEAD**

PAIR OF PLATES

German (Meissen), 1731–1734.

Painted with chinoiserie decoration by Christian Friedrich Herold (c. 1700–c. 1779).

Porcelain; 14¼″ diam. (36.5 cm).

Marked with two crossed swords in blue underglaze.

GERHARD RÖBBIG, MUNICH

PUNCH BOWL

Chinese, for the Western market, Ch'ing Dynasty, early Ch'ien Lung period, c. 1740 A.D.

Famille rose porcelain; 6¾″ H, 15½″ diam. (17, 39.5 cm).

Depicted on one side of the bowl is a youthful Bacchus in a tiger-drawn chariot, surrounded by revelling companions; on the other side, robed figures stand beside a statue of a satyr. Five carp swimming amid seaweed are painted on the inside.

MATTHEW & ELISABETH SHARPE, CONSHOHOCKEN

PAIR OF CHINOISERIE FIGURES

French (Saint-Cloud), c. 1735, Louis XV.

Soft-paste porcelain; 10¾ × 6 × 6″ (27.5 × 15 × 15 cm).

Exhibition: "Les Grands Ébénistes et Menuisiers Parisiens du 18ème Siècle," Musée des Arts Décoratifs, Paris, 1955.

Provenance: L. Allain, Paris.

FREDERICK P. VICTORIA & SON, INC., NEW YORK

THE IMPETUOUS LOVER

German (Meissen), c. 1743.

Model by Johann Joachim Kändler (1706–1775).

Porcelain; 6½ × 7¾ × 5″ (16.5 × 20 × 13 cm).

Similar examples: See K. Berling, *Das Meissner Porzellan und seine Geschichte*, Leipzig, 1900, ill. XXI. Metropolitan Museum of Art, New York (see Y. Hackenbroch, *Meissen and Other Continental Porcelain, The Irwin Untermyer Collection*, Cambridge, Mass., 1956, p. 115, fig. 102, pl. 66); Museum im Kirschgarten, Basel, Pauls Collection (see P.W. Meister, *Porzellan des 18 Jahrhunderts, Die Sammlung Pauls*, Basel, pp. 312–313).

The porcelain group is described as follows in the Meissen factory records (translated from German, see p. 115 Hackenbroch, above): "A group consisting of 4 figures, with a shepherdess seated upon lawn, joined by a finely dressed youth full of amorous intentions but repudiated by her. Riding upon the youth is Cupid, holding him by his hair and hitting his head with a bow, while Harlequin stands nearby in mockery."

GERHARD RÖBBIG, MUNICH

GIOVANNI ANTONIO GUARDI
(1698–1760)

Portrait of the Duke Karl Alexander of Lorraine Wearing the Order of the Golden Fleece

Italian, c. 1735.

Oil on canvas; 27½ × 21" (70 × 53 cm).

Literature: Antonio Morassi, *Atti dell'Accademia di Udine*, 1966–1969, series VII, volume VIII, p. 17; Antonio Morassi, *Antonio e Francesco Guardi I*, p. 330, no. 119; *II*, pl. 141.

Provenance: Field Marshall Johann Matthias von der Schulenberg, inventory no. 149; Private collection, Switzerland.

Duke Karl Alexander, brother of Emperor Franz I, was born in 1712 and became a member of the Order of the Golden Fleece in 1731. The painting seems to be the only known Guardi portrait painted from life, perhaps during a visit by the duke to Venice.

JULIUS BÖHLER, MUNICH

GASPARE TRAVERSI (d. 1769)

The Poet

Italian, c. 1740.

Inscribed: REMISA COLLECTION NO: 314

Oil on canvas; 39¾ × 60¼″ (101 × 153 cm).

Provenance: Duke of Remisa, Madrid; Private collection, Switzerland.

EDWARD SPEELMAN LTD., LONDON

BOX

French (Paris), 1744, Louis XV.

Claude Nicholas Grebeude,
goldsmith; signed.

Gold, mother-of-pearl, shell; $1 \times 2\frac{1}{2} \times 1\frac{1}{2}''$ (2.5 × 6.3 × 3.8 cm).

S. J. PHILLIPS LTD., LONDON

FIGURE OF A KNIFE GRINDER

German (Dresden), c. 1740.

Figure of carved ivory, rose diamonds; wheels of colored glass; frame set with diamonds and rubies; gold and rock crystal base with applied enameled-gold scrollwork, diamonds, rubies; all on a wood base overlaid with two-color amber; 7 × 7½ × 5½″ (18 × 19 × 14 cm).

Similar figure: Pitti Palace, Florence.

Provenance: Mentmore Collection, Buckinghamshire.

D. S. LAVENDER (SOUTH MOLTON ANTIQUES LTD.), LONDON

THE HUNTSMAN WENTZEL WITH THE FAVORITE DOG OF PRINCESS MARIA ANNA OF SAXONY

German (Meissen), 1744.

Model by Johann Joachim Kändler (1706–1775); marked with two blue crossed swords.

Porcelain; 12 × 6″ (30.5 × 15.5 cm).

Similar example: See Dr. K. Berling, *Festschrift zur 200 Jährigen Jubelfeier der Ältesten Europäischen Porzellan-manufaktur Meissen, 1910*, p. 40, fig. 67 (reprinted as *Meissen China: An Illustrated History*, New York, 1972, fig. 67).

This figure is recorded as follows in the Meissen archives (translated from German): "Wentzel 15 inches high in his usual dress exactly resembling him in face and figure, beautifully moulded in clay." Princess Maria Anna was the daughter of August III, Elector of Saxony and King of Poland. She was married to the Elector of Bavaria, Max Joseph.

M. & G. SÉGAL, BASEL

THREE FLOWER VASES

French (Vincennes), 1756, Louis XV.

Marked with interlaced L's and date-letter D; also, incised number 6 or 9.

Soft-paste porcelain; large vase: 8½ × 11 × 6¾" (21.5 × 28 × 17 cm); small vases: 7½ × 7½ × 5¼" (19 × 19 × 13.5 cm).

The vases are in two parts, the foot perforated to allow water to seep into the plant.

EARLE D. VANDEKAR OF KNIGHTSBRIDGE INC., NEW YORK

PAIR OF CHINOISERIE FIGURES

French, mid-eighteenth century,
Louis XV.

Figures of patinated bronze and
three-color lacquer, gilt-bronze socles;
5½ × 5½ × 3″ (14.5 × 14.5 × 8 cm).

ÉTIENNE LÉVY, PARIS

POTPOURRI

Chinese/French.

Chinese porcelain, eighteenth century, Ch'ing Dynasty, possibly K'ang Hsi period, 1662–1722 A.D.

French mount, gilt-bronze, c. 1750, Louis XV.

8 × 7½″ (20.5 × 19 cm).

ÉTIENNE LÉVY, PARIS

WRITING TABLE

English, c. 1770, George III.

Satinwood with kingwood and mahogany inlay; 30¼ × 27 × 16¾" (77 × 68.5 × 42.5 cm).

The right frieze contains a drawer fitted with ink bottles, the front frieze has a leather-top writing surface and blind drawer below. An inlaid musical trophy is depicted on the top surface.

FLORIAN PAPP, INC., NEW YORK

COMMODE

French, c. 1750, Louis XV.

Bernard Van Risenburgh (c. 1700–1765), *ébéniste*.

Stamped: BVRB

Black lacquer, wood, gilt-bronze, brèche d'Alep marble; 35 × 63 × 24¾″ (89 × 160 × 63 cm).

Provenance: Mrs. Robert R. Young,

New York; Private collection, New York.

ROSENBERG & STIEBEL, INC., NEW YORK

SNUFFBOX

English (London), second half of the eighteenth century, George III.

James Cox (flourished 1757–1791), goldsmith; containing a watch in the base, signed by Frederick de Veere, who worked in London from 1769 to 1775.

Gold, agate, diamonds; 2″ H, 3⅞″

diam. (5, 10 cm).

Exhibition: "The Art of the Goldsmith and the Jeweler," A La Vieille Russie, New York, November 1968, cat. no. 141B.

**A LA VIEILLE RUSSIE, INC.,
NEW YORK**

SNUFFBOX

French (Paris), 1778.

Gold, enamel; 1 × 3 × 4¼″ (2.5 × 7.5 × 5.5 cm).

Literature: R. & M. Norton, *A History of Gold Snuff Boxes*, London, 1938, p. 31.

Exhibition: "The Art of the Goldsmith and the Jeweler," A La Vieille Russie, New York, November 1968, cat. no. 99.

The enamel, which includes putti *en grisaille*, is by Charles-Jacques de Mailly (1740–1817), who worked in Moscow in 1775.

A LA VIEILLE RUSSIE, INC., NEW YORK

**CLAUDE-JOSEPH VERNET
(1714–1789)**

The Fishing Monk

French, eighteenth century.

Signed: J. VERNET.

Oil on copper; 11 × 9½″ (28 × 24 cm).

Provenance: Countess Koucheleff; Sale, Hôtel Drouot, Paris, 1875.

The Ferryman (see painting on opposite page) is a companion piece to this work.

**GEMÄLDEGALERIE ABELS,
COLOGNE**

CLAUDE-JOSEPH VERNET (1714–1789)

The Ferryman

French, eighteenth century.

Signed: J. VERNET.

Oil on copper; 11 × 9½″ (28 × 24 cm).

Provenance: Countess Koucheleff; Sale, Hôtel Drouot, Paris, 1875.

The Fishing Monk (see painting on opposite page) is a companion piece to this work.

GEMÄLDEGALERIE ABELS, COLOGNE

CLAUDE-JOSEPH VERNET (1714–1789)

Naufrage (Shipwreck)

French, 1760–1765.

Oil on canvas; 12¾ × 19¾″ (32.4 × 50.2 cm).

Literature: F. Ingersoll-Smouse, *Catalogue raisonné de l'oeuvre peint de Claude-Joseph Vernet*, Paris, 1926, vol. I, p. 93, no. 747, fig. 185.

Provenance: Earl of Elgin, Broomhall, Dumferline, Scotland.

Vue de Marseilles (see painting on opposite page) is a companion piece to this work.

RICHARD L. FEIGEN & CO., NEW YORK

CLAUDE-JOSEPH VERNET (1714–1789)

Vue de Marseille (View of Marseilles)

French, 1768.

Oil on canvas; 12¾ × 19¾″ (32.4 × 50.2 cm).

Literature: F. Ingersoll-Smouse, *Catalogue raisonné de l'oeuvre peint de Claude-Joseph Vernet*, Paris, 1926, vol. I, p. 93, no. 751, fig. 189.

Provenance: Earl of Elgin, Broomhall, Dumferline, Scotland.

Naufrage (see painting on opposite page) is a companion piece to this work.

RICHARD L. FEIGEN & CO., NEW YORK

DRESSING TABLE

American (Philadelphia), c. 1770.

Walnut; 29 × 33¼ × 21″ (73.5 × 84.5 × 53.5 cm).

Provenance: Mitchell Taradash, Philadelphia.

DAVID STOCKWELL, INC., WILMINGTON

HIGHBOY

American (Philadelphia), c. 1750–1770, Chippendale.

Mahogany; 96 × 44 × 23″ (243.8 × 111.8 × 58.4 cm).

Literature: Wallace Nutting, *Furniture Treasury*, Cambridge, Mass., 1928, vol. I., pl. 362; Israel Sack, Inc., New York, *Opportunities in American Antiques*, no. 37, 1982, p. 35, pl. P5203.

Provenance: George S. Palmer, New London, Connecticut (until 1927).

Israel Sack purchased George S. Palmer's home "Westomere" in New London, along with the entire Palmer collection, in 1927.

ISRAEL SACK, INC., NEW YORK

SECRETARY

American (Boston), c. 1760–1765, Chippendale.

Made on order for Jeremiah Lee, Marblehead, Massachusetts.

Mahogany, pine; 97½ × 46½ × 22″ (247.7 × 118.1 × 55.9 cm).

Exhibition: "Reading and Writing," Cooper-Hewitt Museum, New York, 1981–1982.

Provenance: Jeremiah Lee, Marblehead, Massachusetts; Amory family, Massachusetts; Julia Cabot Wilde.

BERNARD & S. DEAN LEVY, NEW YORK

ARMCHAIR

American (Philadelphia), c. 1740,
Queen Anne style.

Walnut; 45¾ × 32¾ × 20¼″ (116 ×
83 × 51.5 cm).

Similar example: Winterthur Museum, Winterthur, Delaware.

Provenance: Biddle family,
Philadelphia.

**DAVID STOCKWELL, INC.,
WILMINGTON**

**FRANÇOIS-HUBERT DROUAIS
(1727–1775)**

Portrait of a Man

French, 1769.

Signed and dated on bookshelf, at center right: DROUAIS 1769.

Oil on canvas; 32¼ × 26⅝" (82 × 62 cm).

Provenance: M. Wildenstein.

**DIDIER AARON, INC.,
NEW YORK**

**DROP-FRONT SECRETARY
(SECRÉTAIRE À
ABATTANT)**

French, c. 1770, Louis XVI.

Joseph Baumhauer (d. 1772),
called "Joseph," *ébéniste*.

Stamped, at top right: JOSEPH.

Purplewood with tulipwood par-
quetry, gilt-bronze, grey marble;
54 × 41 × 15″ (137 × 104 × 38
cm).

Exhibition: "Reading and
Writing," Cooper-Hewitt
Museum, New York, 1981–
1982.

**DIDIER AARON, INC.,
NEW YORK**

PIPE

German (Dresden), c. 1760.

Onyx, gold, ivory, diamonds; 2½″ H, 15½″ L (6.5, 39.5 cm); in fitted case.

Provenance: Presented to the Marquis of Cornwallis by Tippoo Sahib at the surrender of Seringapatam in 1792.

D. S. LAVENDER (SOUTH MOLTON ANTIQUES LTD.), LONDON

BULL

Italian (Rome), seventeenth or eighteenth century; after a Roman marble.

Bronze; 13 × 16¼ × 4¾″ (33 × 41.5 × 12 cm).

Provenance: Otto Wertheimer, Paris.

PAUL ROSENBERG & CO., NEW YORK

PAIR OF CANDLESTICKS

Indian, c. 1780, from a design by English architect Sir William Chambers (1726–1796).

Ivory; 19¼ × 9 × 6½" (49 × 23 × 16.5 cm).

Similar examples: See Nicholas Goodison, *Ormolu: The Work of Matthew Boulton*, London, 1974, figs. 91, 92, which depict Chambers's design and Boulton's candlestick in gilt-bronze; see also Sir William Chambers, *Treatise on the Decorative Part of Civil Architecture*, London, 1759 (3rd edition, London, 1791; reprint 1969), which includes engraving of griffin design under section "Various Ornamental Utensils."

Provenance: Collection of Warren Hastings, first Governor General of India.

WILLIAM REDFORD, LONDON

INKSTAND (ÉCRITOIRE POIRIER)

French (Sèvres), 1776, Louis XV.

Marked with interlaced L's and date-letter Y; also painter's mark C(?) (1?) C.

Soft-paste porcelain, gilt-bronze; 3 × 6¼ × 7″ (7.5 × 16 × 18 cm).

Provenance: René Fribourg, New York.

FREDERICK P. VICTORIA & SON, INC., NEW YORK

MARGUERITE GÉRARD
(1761–1837)

The Piano Lesson

French, 1780s.

Signed, at bottom left: MTE. GÉRARD; dated 1785 or 1786 on the square piano.

Oil on canvas; 18 × 15″ (45.7 × 38.1 cm).

Literature: Ann Sutherland Harris and Linda Nochlin, *Women Artists: 1550–1950*, New York, 1976, cat. no. 64, pp. 199–200, ill. p. 201.

Exhibition: "Women Artists: 1550–1950," 1977. This exhibition appeared at the Los Angeles County Museum of Art; the Carnegie Institute, Pittsburgh; the University of Texas at Austin; and the Brooklyn Museum.

Provenance: Emile Pereire.

H. SHICKMAN GALLERY, NEW YORK

FRANÇOIS-HUBERT DROUAIS
(1727–1775)

Marie-Josephine Louise de Savoie,
Comtesse de Provence

French, c. 1771.

Oil on canvas; 27¼ × 22⅛" (69 × 58 cm).

Literature: Rosenberg & Stiebel, Inc., New York, *European Works of Art III*, 1981, pp. 10–11.

Similar versions: Musée Municipal, Agen; Musée Draguignan.

The Comtesse (1753–1810) was married on May 14, 1771; the Comte de Provence, who was Drouais's protector and gave him the title *Premier Peintre*, presented portraits of his wife as gifts to his friends at court.

ROSENBERG & STIEBEL, INC.,
NEW YORK

137

DROP-FRONT SECRETARY (SECRÉTAIRE À ABATTANT)

French, c. 1780, Louis XVI.

Léonard Boudin (1735–1804), *ébéniste*.

Signed: L. BOUDIN (JME).

Various natural and stained woods—including amaranth, tulipwood, boxwood, and sycamore—over oak, gilt-bronze, brèche d'Alep marble; 54½ × 36 × 16½" (138 × 91 × 42 cm).

Similar example: See Pierre Verlet, *Les Ébénistes du XVIIIème siècle français*, Paris, 1963, p. 121, pl. 4.

DALVA BROTHERS, INC., NEW YORK

COMMODE

French, c. 1775, Louis XV-Louis XVI (Transitional period).

Pierre-Antoine Foullet, *ébéniste* (*maître* 1765).

Signed: P. A. FOULLET (JME).

Various wood veneers—including satinwood, tulipwood, amaranth, boxwood, and sycamore—over oak, gilt-bronze, marble; 34 × 50 × 23½″

(86 × 126 × 60 cm).

Provenance: Victor Rothschild, London (until 1937).

The initials EG and PL in the framed reserves may indicate that the piece was made as a wedding gift.

DALVA BROTHERS, INC., NEW YORK

139

PAIR OF ARMCHAIRS

Chinese, Ch'ing Dynasty, Ch'ien Lung period, 1736–1795 A.D.

Cinnabar lacquer on wood; 37½ × 21¼ × 17¼″ (95 × 54 × 44 cm).

Similar example: E. F. Strange, *Chinese Lacquer*, London, 1926, pl. 23; described as "one of a set of three from the Summer Palace, Peking."

Provenance: Possibly Emperor Ch'ien Lung, Summer Palace, Peking.

The five-clawed dragon carved on the back is rising from the sea and holding aloft the character "shou" ("long life").

DALVA BROTHERS, INC., NEW YORK

INCENSE BURNER (*KORO*)

Chinese, Ch'ing Dynasty, Ch'ien-Lung period, c. 1780 A.D.

Burmese jadeite; 4 × 6⅜″ (10 × 16.5 cm).

Similar example: Avery Brundage Collection, San Francisco.

E & J FRANKEL ORIENTAL ART, NEW YORK

PAIR OF CANDLESTICKS

French, c. 1795–1800, Directoire.

Bronze, gilt-bronze; 14 × 6 × 6″ (35.5 × 15 × 15 cm).

Similar example: See catalogue, collection of M. Jean Bloch, sold in Paris, Palais Galliera, June 1961, no. 75.

The bobêches and basins are in the form of overflowing fountains supported by heads of Neptune; the shafts, applied with gilt-bronze trophies, are supported by three seahorses raised on a plinth, from which emerge fountains.

FREDERICK P. VICTORIA & SON, INC., NEW YORK

TEMPLE-FORM CLOCK

Swiss (Geneva), 1794–1804.

Melchior Monnin (1763–1823), goldsmith.

Signed MELCHIOR MONNIN À GENEVE.

Gold, enamel; with carillon musical movement and singing bird; 9″ H (23 cm).

Exhibition: "The Art of the Goldsmith and the Jeweler," A La Vieille Russie, New York, November 1968, cat. no. 115.

Melchior Monnin was born in France and settled in Geneva in 1793. From 1793 to 1802, he was associated with Antoine Rojard, a firm of watchmakers and jewelers.

**A LA VIEILLE RUSSIE, INC.,
NEW YORK**

COFFEEPOT

Estonian, c. 1770.

Hallmark of city of Reval, Estonia, and maker's mark.

Silver, with wooden handle; 11½ × 6″ (29 × 15 cm).

F. GOREVIC & SON, INC., NEW YORK

144

TANKARD

American (Boston), 1777.

Paul Revere, Jr. (1735–1818), silversmith. With REVERE struck on left of handle and the following inscription engraved on front:

MEMENTO OBT: OCTOBER 1777
BEULAH DANIELSON,
SARAH DANIELSON, MARTHA DANIELSON
LOVELY IN LIFE AND IN
DEATH NOT DIVIDED.

Engraved silver; 9¼" H (23.5 cm); weight: 32 oz.

Provenance: Acquired from a descendant of the original owner.

The women whose names are mentioned in the inscription were the daughters of Timothy Danielson; all three died of the plague. The Danielson family were patrons of Revere (the name is mentioned several times in his daybook).

S. J. SHRUBSOLE CORP., NEW YORK

TEAPOT

American (Boston), c. 1790.

Paul Revere, Jr. (1735–1818), silversmith. Marked on base with a bullet and the inscription REVERE.

Engraved silver, wood handle; 6″ H (15 cm) to top of finial.

Provenance: Direct descent in the Revere family, from Paul Revere to his daughter, Mary Lincoln, to her daughter, to her nephew, to his son, Paul Revere Reynolds.

The initials MJL on the teapot are those of Mary and Jedediah Lincoln, the daughter of Paul Revere and her husband.

FIRESTONE & PARSON, BOSTON

146

JEAN-ANTOINE HOUDON
(1741–1828)

Bust of a Magistrate

French, 1787.

Signed and dated, under right shoulder: HOUDON. F. 1787.

White marble; 25½ × 25 × 12″ (65 × 63 × 31 cm); green marble socle, 6″ H (16 cm).

Literature: Paul Vitry, "La Collection de M. Jacques Doucet," *Les Arts*, September 1903, p. 4., ill.; Gaston Brière, Paul Vitry, et al., "Notes critiques sur les oeuvres de peinture et de sculpture réunies à l'Exposition des Cent Pastels du XVIIIe Siècle ouverte à La Galerie Petite en mai–juin 1908," *Bulletin de la Société de l'histoire de l'art français*, 1908, pp. 167–168; Paul Vitry: "Quelques bustes français à l'exposition des cent pastels," *Revue de l'art ancien et moderne*, July 1908, vol. 24(1), no. 136, p. 25; and "Exposition de cent pastels et de bustes du XVIIIe siècle (review)," *Les Arts*, October 1908, vol. 7, no. 82, p. 2; Georges Giacometti, *Le Statuaire Jean-Antoine Houdon et son époque*, Paris, 1918, vol. I, p. 108; vol. III, pp. 27–28; Louis Réau, *Houdon, sa vie et son oeuvre*, Paris, 1964, vols. III/IV, p. 58, no. 285, pl. CXLV.

Exhibition: "Cent Pastels du XVIIIème Siècle," La Galerie Petite, Paris, May–June 1908, no. 125.

Provenance: Jacques Doucet, Paris, until 1912; S. R. Bertrou, New York; Wilpheimer, New York.

Although the portrait bust has not been positively identified, it may represent M. de Sartine, Minister of State under Louis XVI, or Le Pelletier de Morfontaine, Provost of the Guilds of Paris from 1784 to 1789 (a plaster bust of the latter by Houdon was shown at the Salon of 1785).

FABIUS FRÈRES, PARIS

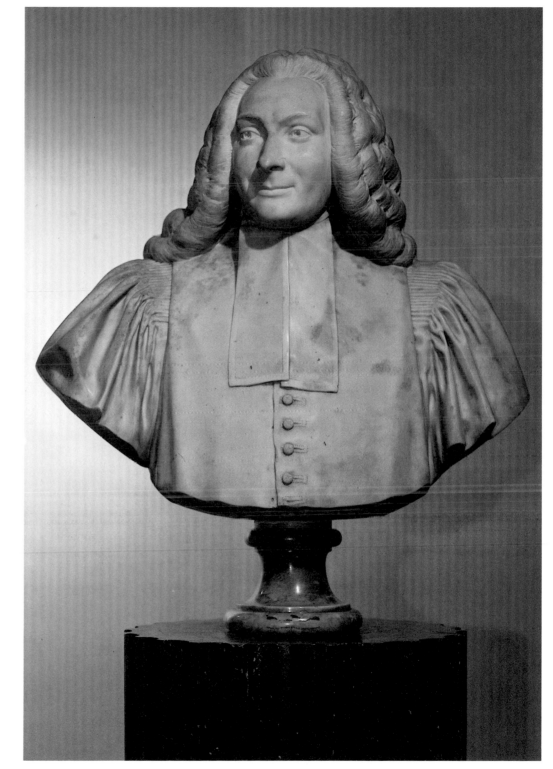

CAMILLE PISSARRO (1830–1903)

Femme et enfant dans les fleurs (Woman and Child Among Flowers)

French, 1879.

Signed and dated, at bottom left.

Oil on canvas; 15 × 18″ (38 × 46 cm).

Literature: Ludovic Rodon Pissarro and Lionello Venturi, *Camille Pissarro, son art, son oeuvre*, Paris, 1939, no. 483.

Exhibitions: "Rétrospective des Oeuvres de C. Pissarro," Galerie Manzi et Joyant, Paris, January–February 1914, no. 82; Tate Gallery, London, June–October 1931, no. 29; Birmingham Museum, October–November 1921, no. 24; Castle Museum, Nottingham, November–December 1931; War Memorial Buildings, Stockport, January 1932, no. 16; Mappin Art Gallery, Sheffield, February–March 1932, no. 18; Sale, Collection C. Pissarro, December 3, 1928, no. 46.

Provenance: Lucien Pissarro, London.

GEMÄLDEGALERIE ABELS, COLOGNE

NINETEENTH CENTURY

King George IV of England was an enthusiast for everything connected with Versailles. As prince regent, and later as king, he collected French art on a scale previously unknown in England, being advised first by Henry Holland and later by Walsh Porter. The situation created by the post-Revolutionary sales of sequestered property of émigrés and Royalists proved advantageous, and George's agents bought extensively when such porcelains, silver, and furniture could be brought to England— the two years 1801 to 1803, when belligerency was suspended during the truce with Napoleon, and later even more lavishly after Napoleon's downfall, when there was no danger to shipping.

For some years after the Revolution, the art market in Paris was in total disarray. Bargains were everywhere. Sir John Dean Paul, a well-known collector who went to Paris in 1802 to buy French furniture, describes how many fine examples were to be found in shabby junk shops whose proprietors would often be seen taking snuff out of magnificent gold boxes. Miss Berry says that Sèvres porcelains were being sold for one-fourth of their original price. An army of dealers and agents invaded France and took what they could. To quote Wordsworth,

> Because the good old rule
> Sufficeth them,—the simple plan,
> That they should take who have the power,
> And they should keep who can.

There were, however, patriotic French art lovers, like the Abbé Grégoire and Alexandre Lenoir, who risked their lives to keep the French from pillaging their own treasures. The abbé wrote a report dated Fructidor 14, Year II, condemning vandalism in France; but basically he agreed with Wordsworth and proved himself delighted with the looting of other countries: he praised the methodical robbery by the Revolutionary armies in Italy and then took part in the festival held in Paris to mark the reception of the stolen Italian works of art.

Lenoir was a more admirable character, who risked his life and broke laws to save what he could of the French cultural heritage. He covered the bronze figures from the Condé tombs with glue, to protect them from looters, and in his efforts to rescue the tomb of Cardinal Richelieu from destruction by soldiers, he received a bayonet wound in his hand. He had a passion to preserve every surviving vestige of the past, but on the whole his efforts—like those of the Abbé Grégoire—were ineffective. Vandalism wiped out a great deal of French art.

A frenzied interest in the art market resulted from the Orléans and Versailles sales and from the collecting activities of Catherine the Great of Russia and Frederick the Great of Germany. Everywhere, paintings were sold feverishly, and prices rose constantly. According to Farington, George III remarked, "I know not how it is, but I never sent a *gentleman* in a public capacity to Italy, but he came back a picture dealer."

CONTINUED ON PAGE 153

JAN FRANS VAN DAEL
(1764–1840)

An Arrangement of Flowers

Flemish, 1801.

Signed and dated, at lower right: VAN DAEL AN 9 (year 9, or 1801, in the Revolutionary Calendar of France).

Oil on canvas; 24 × 19½″ (61 × 50 cm).

Provenance: Member of the Bonaparte family, Paris; Private collection, Paris.

Van Dael left his native Antwerp for Paris in 1736 and became a favorite of Napoleon Bonaparte and his wife Josephine. He died in Paris.

NEWHOUSE GALLERIES, INC., NEW YORK

PAIR OF DISHES

English (Derby), c. 1810.

Decorated by Philip Clavey; gilding
in the main by Gilder Talkington.

Marked with crown, with D and cross
in red; also, marked with number 29
in yellow, number 4 in yellow, and
number 36 in red.

Porcelain; 8 × 9″ (20.5 × 23 cm).

**EARLE D. VANDEKAR OF
KNIGHTSBRIDGE INC.,
NEW YORK**

TEA AND COFFEE SERVICE

German (Meissen), c. 1815.

Each covered piece marked with underglaze blue crossed-swords mark, numeral I.

White biscuit porcelain; top right, covered teapot, 7″ H (18 cm); top center, covered coffeepot, 11″ H (28 cm); top right, covered sugar bowl, 7″ H (18 cm); bottom left and right, covered coffeepots, 10″ H (25.4 cm); bottom center, cup and saucer, 3½″ H (9 cm).

The pieces are in the Wedgewood style with allegorical gold cameos and gilded griffin spout on covered items.

FLEUR-DE-LIS ANTIQUES, PALM BEACH

The greatest of these British "picture dealers," William Buchanan, a Scottish lawyer, never went to Italy, however. He did have an agent in Rome, James Irvine, who was an assiduous purchaser of pictures, but the treasures he sought were not always easy to acquire. Once, after long negotiations to obtain an altar painting by Domenichino, the villagers learned they were about to lose their altarpiece and threatened to tear down the church and kill anyone who tried to remove the painting. Irvine abandoned the project, and Buchanan lost considerable money on the deal. Other purchases worked out better, but there was always the risk that ships might be seized by the French. In spite of all the difficulties, it is amazing that a torrent of masterpieces crossed the Channel and were eagerly acquired by peers as well as by rich bankers and merchants such as Angerstein, the Hopes, and the Barings.

Buchanan realized what any able dealer knows—that real power resides less in collectors than in their advisers, who are mostly artists. To use Buchanan's blunt words, it was necessary to bribe these advisers. The first to be procured was the president of the Royal Academy, Benjamin West, who was characterized by the dealer as "Doctor West, that learned and enlightened quack, who has the address to make some folks believe that white is black, and au contraire, Black, White." West was not the only recipient of Buchanan's largesse. The dealer bestowed his favors upon a whole group of Royal Academicians: Lawrence, adviser to Angerstein; Cosway, to the Marquess of Stafford; Tresham, to Beckford and Sir Richard Worsley; and Walton, to Lord Fitzwilliam. All these distinguished artists, who were looked on as the "experts" of their day, were in one way or another subsidized, just as many "experts" have been ever since.

Because many Italian families were ruined by Napoleon's taxes, Italian dealers were given the opportunity to buy from the nobility. Among these merchants were the Camuccini brothers, who owned such masterpieces as the *Feast of the Gods* by Bellini and Titian, and *Bacchus and Ariadne* by Titian. Their collection was bought *in toto* by the Duke of Northumberland, and at his estate, Alnwick, many of these pictures can still be seen.

The French controlled Italy and looted it to establish the Musée Napoléon at the Louvre under Vivant-Denon. Most of these stolen works of art, the greatest assemblage ever brought together, were returned after Napoleon's defeat. This temporary pillage for national use, however, meant that French private collectors gathered much less than Buchanan and other English dealers shipped home. It is not a coincidence that the two outstanding French private collectors, Cardinal Fesch and Lucien Bonaparte, were both related to Napoleon—being his uncle and younger brother respectively—though they were not always on good terms with him.

There was also looting for private collections in Spain. King Joseph, another brother of Napoleon, fled from Spain with five pictures attributed to Raphael. General Murat, then governor of Madrid, acquired many of the great Renaissance masterpieces previously stolen by Godoy, the Prince of Peace. Even the Danish minister in those troubled times managed to acquire Raphael's *Alba Madonna*, while Marshal Soult helped himself to Titians, Van Dycks, and especially Murillos. Buchanan had his agent, George Augustus Wallis, on the spot. Wallis remained loyally on duty in spite of danger and, according to Buchanan's diary, "profited by [political] changes to acquire works of art for this country [England], endeavoring always, as a professional man and artist, to stand well with all parties."

Slightly earlier than Buchanan, Consul Smith was another English dealer of note. His major patron was George III, though he was also the purveyor of art to several peers. Smith settled in Venice and was soon appointed consular officer. This position

WRITING SET (ÉCRITOIRE)

French, 1815–1820, Restoration.

Gold, diamonds, emeralds, sapphires, rubies, turquoise, pearls.

The set includes box, seal, pair of ink boxes, sealing wax case, bookmark, pen, and pencil.

**JAMES ROBINSON INC.,
NEW YORK**

had its advantages, for the consulate functioned as the bank for young English milords making the Grand Tour. Smith's first wife introduced him to painters, and his second to her brother, the King's Resident. Thus Smith became the bridge between visiting Englishmen and contemporary Venetian artists. For twenty-five years, he acted as business manager for Canaletto and sold George III fifty-three paintings by the Venetian master. He also placed additional canvases in the homes of many peers. And he provided English collectors with works by Bellini, Veronese, and other Renaissance masters.

A wealthy English timber merchant, Edward Solly, lived in Berlin throughout the Napoleonic Wars. When he began collecting in 1811, he was in a position to buy great masterpieces of the High Renaissance comparable to those that had been flowing into London. But, unlike his London counterparts, he also owned four panels from Van Eyck's Ghent altarpiece and paintings by Rogier van der Weyden and other fifteenth-century Flemings. His acquisitions of Italian art went beyond the High Renaissance. He was probably the first to collect Quattrocento painters, such as Botticelli and Andrea del Castagno, extensively. Few were the connoisseurs in Europe at that time who would even have heard their names. Was Solly therefore a pioneer in the appreciation of earlier artists? The answer is obscure, as most of his pictures were bought by agents. It is doubtful that he even went to Italy, and certainly he did not travel there a great deal. Even his judgments in art were scarcely his own. He submitted his proposed purchases to a committee of Berlin art-history professors, much as Norton Simon used to ask the advice of several museum directors before acquiring a painting—and, like Norton Simon, he assembled one of the great collections of his time. When his ships carrying timber to England were seized by Napoleon and he

faced financial ruin, Solly managed, after endless negotiations, to sell all his works of art (more than 3,000 items) to the Prussian state, where they formed what came to be the nucleus of the Kaiser Friedrich Museum. In 1821, Solly moved to England, gave up the timber business, and became an art dealer. His sales were not impressive, but they kept him comfortable.

After the Napoleonic Wars, a temporary recession in art dealing took place on the Continent. Notable collections were formed, but the art market itself was sluggish. It is all the more remarkable, therefore, that a French dealer with an English name, John Arrowsmith, launched in Paris an underrated English painter, John Constable. This came about somewhat accidentally. Géricault attended the annual Royal Academy banquet as a guest and, on returning to Paris, told his friends that he was astounded by the beauty and originality of Constable's paintings and equally amazed that he was not a full member of the Academy. The next year, to Constable's surprise, Arrowsmith arrived at his studio. After considerable bargaining, the French dealer agreed to pay £250 for *The Hay Wain, View on the Stour*, and a small study of Yarmouth. The pictures were shown in Arrowsmith's shop, and as Constable wrote, "My pictures in the Gallery at Paris went off with great *éclat*," and at the Salon of 1824 he received a gold medal. For a time his *réclame* in France was considerable. The critics were generous, and his pictures sold well. Another French dealer, Claude Schroth, visited him and ordered more pictures. At a time when he badly needed money, Constable managed to sell more than twenty landscapes in France, more than he sold in England during his entire life. Although the depression caused Arrowsmith to go bankrupt and Schroth to withdraw from the market, this story is a splendid example of how dealers can rescue a great painter from the indifference of native collectors, a feat

PIERRE-AUGUSTE RENOIR (1841-1919)

Baigneuse nue assise (Nude Bather Seated)

French, c. 1885–1890.

Signed, at bottom left: A RENOIR

Red chalk, heightened with white; 14½ × 11″ (37 × 28 cm).

Literature: A. Vollard: *Tableaux, pastels et dessins de Pierre-Auguste Renoir*, Paris, 1918, vol. I, ill. p. 37, pl. 145; and *En écoutant Cézanne, Degas, Renoir*, Paris, 1938, ill. after p. 224; John Rewald, *Renoir Drawings*, New York, 1946, pl. 21, no. 56, ill.

Provenance: Jacques Dubourg; César de Hauke; Mrs. Erskine-Mange; Private collection, England.

GALERIE BRAME ET LORENCEAU, PARIS

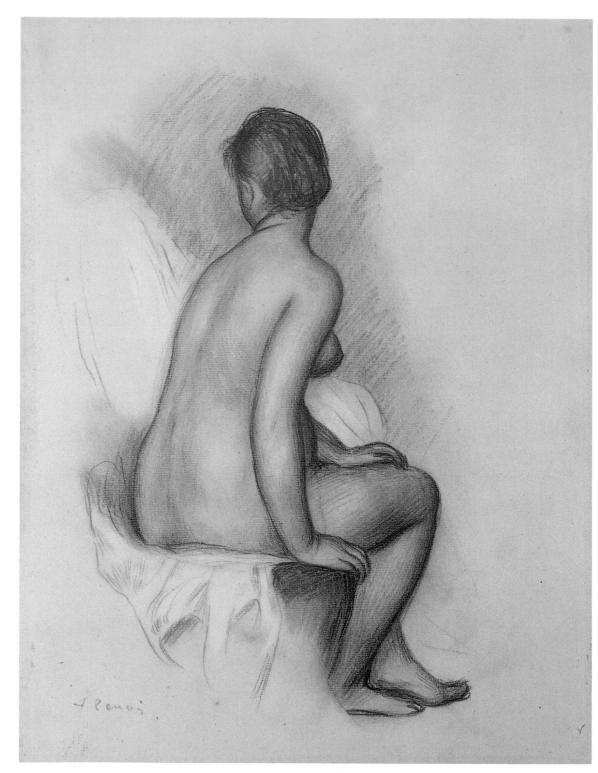

156

we shall see again with Durand-Ruel and the Impressionists.

One English print dealer, Colnaghi's, did help Constable to some extent. The oldest English company continuously dealing in art, Colnaghi's was founded in 1760 by Giovanni Battista Torre, who opened a store in Paris primarily for the sale of scientific instruments. A few years later, he occupied a second shop in Market Lane, near Pall Mall. There, he practiced pyrotechnics and sold prints on the side. Whenever it was not banned by the police, the sale of fireworks was a goldmine; and even when it was forbidden it seems likely that Torre, under the counter and with discretion, continued to dispense rockets, Roman candles, pinwheels, and so on. The print business, if less profitable, was also less explosive—and it was legitimate, after all. In the end, print publishing proved to be remunerative enough, especially after a connection with Bartolozzi was established, so that the sale of fireworks was gradually abandoned and Colnaghi's became purely a firm of art dealers.

When Constable, with the help of Lucas, prepared a volume of his mezzotints, *English Landscape*, for publication, it was logical to turn for distribution to the leading print dealer: Paul Colnaghi, who had taken over the firm from Torre, his distant relative. Constable's sales, however, were disappointing, and the venture was a complete failure. The painter entered an amusing note in his *Journal* when the firm was on the verge of bankruptcy: "I hear there is quite a bustle at Colnaghi's. They are all breaking up.... Dominic is said to make love to all the ladies who look over prints there.... Old Colnaghi is so fond of birds that he has nearly a dozen in his room."

In spite of young Colnaghi's lubricity and his father's aviary, the firm limped along. The hatred of one Colnaghi son for his sibling proved expensive; they often expressed their mutual dislike by bidding against one another at auctions, much to their parent's chagrin. It was not until this century that the firm assumed considerable significance. Under the guidance of O. C. H. Gutekunst and Gustavus Mayer, prints and drawings were somewhat subordinated to paintings. (The new partners were a formidable pair, and with Matthiessen and Knoedler's they formed a syndicate to buy the paintings offered on Stalin's order from the Hermitage Gallery. Second only to the Orléans sales, this was probably the greatest single transaction in the history of art dealing.)

So far we have discussed only true merchants of art. One class of dealer that has always existed but that we have not specifically mentioned is the *marchand amateur*. Many of the collectors already discussed could be placed in this category, but to clarify the distinction, consider Sir Thomas Baring. His father, Sir Francis Baring, built the family fortune, was Pitt's "commercial oracle in the House of Commons," and had garnered immense riches as a merchant banker. His two sons, Sir Thomas and Alexander, inherited this vast wealth. In spite of his wealth, Sir Thomas was a typical *marchand amateur*, selling his *Madonna della Tenda* by Raphael —only one year after purchasing it himself—to the heir of the Bavarian throne, a sale that shocked all English art lovers. This was one of a number of sales Sir Thomas made, but at the same time he bought extensively, particularly from Le Brun, who should be classified not as an *amateur* but as a true *marchand*.

When Sir Thomas died, he left a great collection that was bought in by his son, also named Thomas. A still more ardent collector, the second Thomas added to the family holdings by acquiring the largest share, forty-three pictures, from the most famous Dutch private collection, that of Baron Verstolk. Until he died, the second Sir Thomas, who was not a *marchand amateur*, continued to

CONTINUED ON PAGE 161

157

ALEXANDRE-GABRIEL DECAMPS (1803–1860)

Duck Shooting

French, c. 1828–1829.

Signed, at lower right: DECAMPS.

Oil on canvas; 14 × 18½″
(35.6 × 47 cm).

Literature: Dewey F. Mosby,
*Alexandre-Gabriel Decamps 1803–
1860*, New York, 1977, vol. II,
p. 494, no. 205, pl. 14B.

Provenance: Thomas J. Bryan;
The New-York Historical Society.

The painting is one of a series of at
least four hunting scenes, another of
which can be seen on the opposite
page.

**RICHARD L. FEIGEN & CO.,
NEW YORK**

ALEXANDRE-GABRIEL DECAMPS (1803–1860)

The Fox Chase

French, c. 1828–1829.

Signed on log, lower center: DECAMPS.

Oil on canvas; 14 × 18½″
(35.6 × 47 cm).

Literature: Dewey F. Mosby,
  *Alexandre-Gabriel Decamps 1803–
  1860*, New York, 1977, vol. II,
  p. 494, no. 206, pl. 15B.

Provenance: Thomas J. Bryan;
  The New-York Historical Society.

The painting is one of a series of at
least four hunting scenes, another of
which can be seen on the opposite
page.

**RICHARD L. FEIGEN & CO.,
NEW YORK**

JOHN FREDERICK HERRING, SR. (1795–1865)

A Gray Hunter in Windsor Forest

English, 1828.

Signed and dated, at lower right, on tree trunk: J.F. HERRING 1828.

Oil on canvas; 22⅛ × 30″ (56.2 × 76.2 cm).

Provenance: Mrs. Taylor, London.

RICHARD L. FEIGEN & CO., NEW YORK

acquire in almost every field, including Spanish, early Netherlandish, and French Rococo. This diversity is worth mentioning because it shows an important change in fashion. Taste had become less rigid, and connoisseurs felt they could hang primitives, Rococo paintings, and the established Dutch and Italian masters side by side.

Along with *marchands amateurs*, there have also been those who might be termed *scholar dealers*. I have mentioned Le Brun, but a far more important scholar among art dealers was Théophile Thoré, who was born in 1807. To him we owe the reconstruction of the *oeuvre* of Vermeer. Le Brun knew of Vermeer's existence from the signature on the Rothschild *Astronomer*, already mentioned, but no one had followed up this clue to disentangle Vermeer's works from those of other Dutch artists to whom his pictures had been attributed. Thoré's masterly publication in the *Gazette des Beaux-Arts* in 1866 accomplished this, and in so doing provided a model for future monographs. His dealings in Dutch art furnished him a livelihood, but the sales he made were unimportant compared to his brilliant work as an art historian. All lovers of art are in his debt for their enjoyment of one of the great masters who might otherwise have been forgotten.

To another dealer, Paul Durand-Ruel, we owe to some extent the survival of a whole school of painting that has become a major delight to modern collectors. With the small amount of money inherited from his father, who was also a dealer, Durand-Ruel financed a group of young and unrecognized artists, who eventually became known as the Impressionists. After their rejection by the Salon, he helped organize their exhibitions, promoted their sales, lent them money, and tried his best to force their work on customers who had come to buy Bouguereau and Jules Breton. All this he did with the contempt of the press, the Academy, and other

painters. Twice he was on the verge of bankruptcy. In desperation, he hoped that America would be more adventuresome in taste and opened a New York gallery. Aided by the artist Mary Cassatt, he did find sales in the New World that helped to sustain him.

Although the sums Paul Durand-Ruel paid Manet, Monet, Morisot, Pissarro, Renoir, and Sisley were picayune, these pittances enabled those without private means to eat. In an effort to drive him out of the market, the other picture dealers formed a coalition. They bought a stock of Impressionist canvases and put them up for sale, unframed, hoping that low auction prices would ruin their hated rival and terminate the careers of the painters he had befriended. But Durand-Ruel survived. Although at one time he was in debt for more than a million gold francs and was relatively poor when he died, he had in stock 1,500 pictures by Degas, Renoir, Pissarro, and other despised Impressionists.

Thomas Agnew was another dealer who helped contemporary artists. His original place of business was in Manchester, where the founder of his firm, Vittore Zanetti, had set up as a general *antiquaire* early in the century. At that time, art dealing was insufficiently profitable, just as it had been for Gersaint, Torre, and others, and Zanetti diversified his stock, selling artist's materials, fabricating mirrors, and making meteorological instruments. Pictures were the least important part of the firm's business until after Zanetti's death, when Agnew, his young partner, took over. The new owner began promoting living artists aggressively. *The Art-Journal* wrote in 1861, "The principal support of British art proceeds from wealthy Lancashire. Some twenty years ago, the merchants and manufacturers there were collectors of 'old masters.' They paid large sums of money for 'names' with bad pictures. Of late, however, fabrications of Titians and Raphaels made no sales in that district. Undoubtedly

ASHER BROWN DURAND (1796–1886)

View in the Catskills

American, 1844, Hudson River School.

Signed, at lower left: A.B. DURAND 1844.

Oil on canvas; 37¾ × 54" (95.9 × 137.2 cm).

Literature: Charles C. Cunningham, "American Landscapes," *MFA Bulletin*, 1938, XXXVI, no. 215, p. 39, fig. 1, erroneously dated 1847; *American Paintings in the Museum of Fine Arts, Boston*, Boston, 1969, Vol. I, p. 98, no. 362, Vol. II, p. 196, fig. 304; David B. Lawall, *Asher B. Durand*, New York, 1978, p. 47, no. 93, fig. 46.

Exhibitions: National Academy of Design, New York, 1845, no. 175; American Art-Union, New York, 1845, no. 28; "Century of American Landscape," Carnegie Institute, Pittsburgh, 1939; "The Hudson River School and the Early American Landscape Tradition," Whitney Museum of American Art, New York, 1945, p. 44, no. 102, ill.; "A. B. Durand, 1796–1886," Montclair Art Museum, New Jersey, October–November 1971, no. 48.

Provenance: American Art-Union, New York; R. H. Messenger, New York; Charles D. White, New York (1936); Museum of Fine Arts, Boston.

BERRY-HILL GALLERIES, INC., NEW YORK

the change was mainly affected by the judgement and taste of Mr. Agnew." The wealth accumulated toward the middle of the nineteenth century by Manchester merchants gave a strong impetus to art collecting. With signed paintings by living artists in their possession, these inexperienced collectors felt safer than with dubious Old Masters; but their evaluation of contemporary art seems odd. Maclise's *Sleeping Beauty*, for instance, was valued at nearly three times a Turner masterpiece, *Mortlake Terrace*, now in the National Gallery of Art in Washington. This was in 1851, the year England's greatest painter died. The inventory of living artists sold in the nineteenth century by Agnew's contains few names still remembered. Thomas's son, William, who next headed the firm, was well advised to abandon contemporary art and turn to the Old Masters, even though a British painter lamented:

Those happy days long fled
When William Agnew fed
Not wholly on the dead.

But William fed voraciously on many of the greatest masterpieces ever brought to England, most of which eventually reached America.

Agnew and Durand-Ruel both supported contemporary artists, but the English firm helped the inept and the French firm the gifted. And although William Agnew's contemporary artists were incompetent, he made a fortune; although Paul Durand-Ruel's painters were geniuses, he did not.

In the United States, meanwhile, art dealing had begun. Samuel Putnam Avery was one of the first to sell professionally. He resembled Thomas Agnew rather than Paul Durand-Ruel, in that his acquisitions of contemporary painters were tasteless but salable. And although Avery has been memorialized by the Metropolitan Museum, the artists whose work he sold have been for the most part totally forgotten. His rich customers knew nothing about art, and he was incapable of enlightening them. Nevertheless, Avery was an important personage on the art scene, largely because he seems to have gained considerable wealth in some way. Judging by the prices paid at the many auctions held by Avery —1,561 pictures averaged less than $250—he could scarcely have become rich as an art dealer. It was his good fortune, however, to have as a close friend William T. Walters of Baltimore, who probably shared with Avery many of his highly profitable business interests. A dealer with impressive private wealth has always held strong appeal to Americans (see, for example, Lord Duveen). Money, they think, is an indication of reliability. According to the American ethos, the two have always been in close conjunction, and reliability is what the collector most values.

Avery was rich enough to be a "joiner." He belonged to twenty-four organizations—artistic, philanthropic, scientific, and educational—as well as numerous social clubs. This meant that he had many friends, some of whom he could involve in his pet project, a museum for New York City. In 1869, when the first meeting of the Union League Club's art committee took place to discuss the establishment of the Metropolitan Museum, Avery was named secretary. Later, the committee met in Avery's "Art Rooms"; and when the museum was established in 1870, he was elected a trustee and became the principal adviser to the board on art matters. Whether it is desirable for a museum to have a dealer advising its purchases is debatable, and such a debate raged many years later when Duveen became a trustee of the National Gallery in London. Judging by the works Avery sold, his recommendations to the Metropolitan must have been deplorable. A published cartoon showed him on the prow of a ship holding a banner with the names of the painters he was bringing from Europe:

CONTINUED ON PAGE 176

163

PAIR OF JEWEL CHESTS

Russian, 1839.

Carl Johann Tegelsten (1798–1852), silversmith, a Finn who worked in Russia for Nichols & Plinke. Russian hallmark with date 1839 and maker's mark.

Silver; 6½ × 9½ × 7½"
(16.5 × 24 × 19 cm).

These chests were part of the wedding gifts to Maria Nicholaevna, daughter of Nicholas I. They were presented to her either by her father or her brother, the future Alexander II. Her monogram and a crown appear on one side, the imperial cipher on the other.

**F. GOREVIC & SON, INC.,
NEW YORK**

HOT-WATER URN

Chinese, made for the Western market, c. 1840.

Marked кнс (for Khecheong, a silversmith whose shop was on Club Street, Canton).

Silver; 13¾″ H (35 cm).

Exhibition: Metropolitan Museum of Art, New York.

Similar example: See H. A. Crosby Forbes, J. D. Kernan, and R. S. Wilkins, *Chinese Export Silver, 1785–1885*, Milton, Mass., 1975, fig. 103, no. 298.

Provenance: Ferdinand H. Davis.

Prototypes for this model can be found in English silver.

RALPH M. CHAIT GALLERIES, INC., NEW YORK

PAIR OF GOAT TUREENS

Chinese, made for the Western
market, c. 1840.

Hard-paste porcelain, metal handles;
7″ H, 15″ L (18, 38 cm).

The tureens are decorated all over
with a Chinese town scene and city
wall, probably representing Canton.

**STAIR & COMPANY INC.,
NEW YORK**

GARDEN CARPET

Northwest Persian
(Bakhshayesh),
mid-nineteenth century.

Wool, cotton; 129 × 100″
(327.5 × 254 cm).

**VOJTECH BLAU INC.,
NEW YORK**

JEAN-BAPTISTE-CAMILLE COROT (1796–1875)

Portrait of a Young Woman

French, 1868–1872.

Signed, at upper right: COROT.

Oil on canvas; 12⅞ × 9⅝″ (32.5 × 24.5 cm).

Literature: Julius Meier-Graefe, *Corot*, Berlin, 1930, pl. CXXIV.

Exhibitions: Knoedler Gallery, Paris, 1921; Valentine Dudensing, 1929; "Corot and Daumier," The Museum of Modern Art, New York, October–November 1930, no. 33, ill.; "Corot," Philadelphia Museum of Art, 1946, no. 57, ill.

Provenance: Dr. F. H. Hirschland, New York.

STEPHEN HAHN, INC., NEW YORK

JEAN-BAPTISTE-CAMILLE COROT (1796–1875)

Judith

French, 1872–1874.

Stamped in red, at lower right: VENTE COROT.

Oil on canvas; 41½ × 24½" (105.5 × 62 cm).

Literature: A. Robaut, *L'oeuvre de Corot*, Paris, 1905, vol. III, p. 295, no. 2141, ill.; *Les Arts*, Paris, September 1908, ill. p. 12; P. Goujon, "Corot, Peintre de Figures," *Gazette des Beaux-Arts*, Paris, 1909, vol. II, p. 480; C. Bernheim de Villers, *Corot, peintre de figures*, Paris, 1930, no. 313, ill.; Julius Meier-Graefe, *Corot*, Berlin, 1930, pl. CXLVI.

Exhibitions: "A Century of French Painting," M. Knoedler & Co., Inc., New York, November–December 1928, no. 3; "Corot and Daumier," The Museum of Modern Art," New York, October–November 1930, no. 35, ill.; "Corot," Philadelphia Museum of Art, 1946, no. 69, ill.; "Corot," Art Institute of Chicago, October–November 1960, no. 139; "Corot and Courbet," David Carritt Limited, London, June–July 1979, no. 13, ill. p. 37.

Provenance: Vente Posthume Corot, 1875, no. 206; M. Surville; Dr. Seymour, Paris, 1888; Sale, Hôtel Drouot, Paris, May 29, 1897, no. 17; Paul Gallimard, Paris, 1903; William Ottman, New York; Galerie Etienne Bignou, Paris; Germain Seligman, New York.

E. V. THAW & CO., INC., NEW YORK

PENDANT

English, 1855–1865, Victorian, Renaissance Revival style.

Gold, diamond, ruby, enamel; 3″ L (7.5 cm).

JAMES ROBINSON INC., NEW YORK

PORTRAIT PENDANT

Italian, c. 1860–1865.

Castellani, maker; marked twice on the back with pair of interlocking c's.

Emerald, gold, enamel, ruby, diamonds, pearl; 3″ L (7.5 cm).

A LA VIEILLE RUSSIE, INC., NEW YORK

BRACELET

Austrian, 1850–1860, Francis Joseph I.

Gold, enamel; set with emeralds,
amethyst, peridot, topaz, garnet.

**JAMES ROBINSON INC.,
NEW YORK**

BOX

Austrian (Vienna), 1875.

Hermann Ratzersdorfer, goldsmith. With maker's mark and Austrian hallmark for Vienna 1876.

Silver-gilt, enamel, lapis lazuli, rock crystal; 4×6¼×4¾″ (10×16×12 cm).

The central plaques depict the signs of the zodiac.

F. GOREVIC & SON, INC., NEW YORK

173

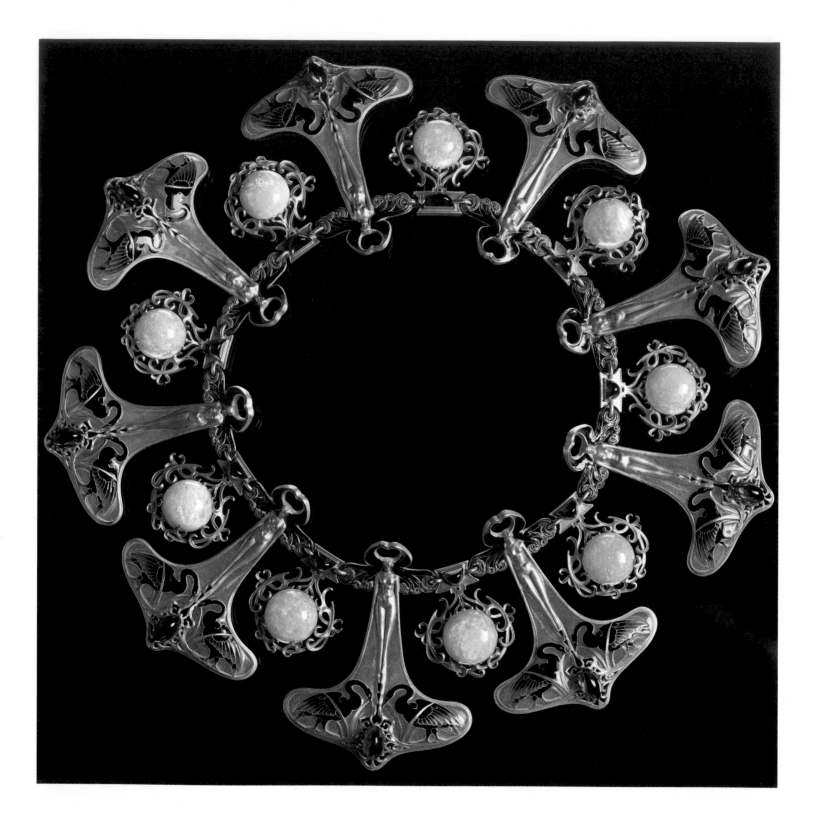

◄ NECKLACE

French, c. 1897–1899, Art Nouveau.

René Lalique (1860–1945), gold-smith.

Signed: LALIQUE.

Gold, enamel, Australian opals, amethysts.

Literature: A. Quantin, *L'Exposition du siècle*, Paris, 1900, p. 110, ill.; H. Vever, *La bijouterie française au XIXème siècle*, Paris, 1908, vol. III, p. 735, ill.; D. Janson, *From Slave to Siren*, Durham, N.C., 1971, cat. no. 165, pl. 19; K. McClinton, *Lalique for Collectors*, New York, 1975, p. 56, ill.; S. Barten, *René Lalique 1890–1900: Schmuck und Objets d'Art*, Munich, 1977, p. 244, fig. 341; Marc and Marie-Claude Lalique, *Lalique par Lalique*, Paris, 1977, p. 41, ill.

Exhibition: Paris Universal Exposition, 1900; "From Slave to Siren," Duke University Museum of Art, Durham, North Carolina, 1971.

LILLIAN NASSAU LTD., NEW YORK

VASE ►

English, late nineteenth century.

Thomas Webb & Sons, maker.

Cameo carved glass; 10½″ H (26.5 cm).

Literature: Ray and Lee Grover, *English Cameo Glass*, New York, 1980, p. 414, fig. C407.

LILLIAN NASSAU LTD., NEW YORK

Escosura, Vibert, Schreyer, Cabanel, Madrazo, Boughton, and Detaille, a lamentable cargo of artists as forgotten, until recently, as those sponsored at about the same time by the Agnews.

Avery's firm has vanished, but another established shortly before the beginning of his career still continues. In 1846, Michel Knoedler came to New York as the representative of Goupil, a French company specializing in engravings. At that time, there were few American collectors of any significance. In the 1850s, Knoedler managed to persuade a collector to pay $300 for a painting. Immediately after this sale, he wrote his firm in Paris expressing doubts that any painting would ever again fetch such a large price in New York! Given this conviction, he must have been remarkably courageous to buy out the Goupil interests in 1857. The Civil War was yet to come, and sales were few and far between.

But Michel Knoedler *was* a man of courage. Moreover, he seems to have had a good eye for contemporary American art. His firm discovered and sold the work of George Caleb Bingham, one of America's great painters. As early as 1852, Bingham wrote a letter offering to send a daguerreotype of *Canvassing for Votes*, which Knoedler had commissioned so that he would have an idea of the "grouping, expression, etc." From the beginning, therefore, M. Knoedler and Co. was involved with contemporary American painting of a quality superior to Avery's mediocre artists. Winslow Homer, for example, sold only to Knoedler's, although he was not always happy with their salesmanship. He once wrote that he would refuse to paint another picture until a purchaser had been found for the last he had consigned, a stimulating challenge to any dealer.

With the end of the Civil War, Michel Knoedler's problems diminished. With the rise in prosperity, the arts became more popular. Nevertheless, when Andrew Mellon went to Europe as a young man and returned to Pittsburgh with a picture for which he had paid $1,000, his friends were astonished that a man of such obvious business sagacity should have been so foolishly extravagant. His father, a few years earlier, had sent a credit investigator from his bank to determine the advisability of making a loan to Henry Clay Frick. He received the following report: "Lands good, ovens well built, manager on job all day, keeps books evenings, may be a little too enthusiastic about pictures but not enough to hurt."

For an art dealer in the 1870s, America must have seemed—to use an idiom of many of the future clients of M. Knoedler and Co.—a "dry hole." Yet Knoedler drilled on, and his patience and faith in the United States were rewarded. The Museum of Fine Arts in Boston and The Metropolitan Museum of Art in New York were both established in 1870; and though their collections remained mediocre for many years, a wave of interest in collecting was about to sweep across the country. The art business was slowly expanding and, with great daring, Michel Knoedler moved up to Fifth Avenue at Twenty-second Street in 1869. Prices moved up with him: a Jules Breton brought $7,500 and a Gérôme $13,500. In roughly twenty years, a top price for a painting in New York had risen forty-five-fold, from $300 to $13,500!

New collectors soon swarmed to M. Knoedler and Co., as the firm was christened when Roland Knoedler became a partner. Among these early buyers were Ogden Mills, M. C. D. Borden, Catharine Lorillard Wolfe, Collis P. Huntington, and John Jacob Astor. Museums also entered the market. For a time the Corcoran Gallery in Washington was a leading customer, but other galleries with larger endowments soon pushed it aside. Such museum competition has made dealers prosperous, just as their continuing quest for masterpieces has made great museums possible.

CONTINUED ON PAGE 187

**GEORGE COCHRAN LAMBDIN
(1830–1896)**

Calla Lilies

American, 1874.

Signed, at lower right: GEO. C. LAMBDIN
1874.

Oil on panel; 20×12″(50.9×30.2 cm).

**BERRY-HILL GALLERIES, INC.,
NEW YORK**

HENRI THÉODORE FANTIN-LATOUR (1836–1904)

Fleurs et fruits (Flowers and Fruit)

French, 1876.

Signed, at upper left: FANTIN 76.

Oil on canvas; 13×18″ (33×45.5 cm).

Literature: Madame Fantin-Latour,

Catalogue de l'oeuvre complet de Fantin-Latour, Paris, 1911, p. 86, no. 792.

Exhibition: "Important XIX and XX Century Works of Art," Alex Reid & Lefevre Ltd., London, July 1981, no. 11, ill. p. 25.

Provenance: Galloway, London, 1905; D. A. Donlap, Canada; Cooling Galleries, Toronto; John A. MacAulay, Toronto; Private collection, California.

HIRSCHL & ADLER GALLERIES, NEW YORK

HENRI-THÉODORE FANTIN-LATOUR (1836–1904)

Panier de fleurs (Basket of Flowers)

French, 1892.

Signed and dated, at upper left: FANTIN 92.

Oil on canvas; 24½ × 31½″ (62 × 80 cm).

Literature: Madame Fantin-Latour, *Catalogue de l'oeuvre complet de Fantin-Latour*, Paris, 1911, p. 156, no. 1481.

Exhibitions: "Exposition Rétrospective de l'Oeuvre de Fantin-Latour," Palais des Beaux Arts, Paris, 1906, cat. no. 90; "Exposition du Centenaire de la Naissance de Fantin-Latour," Musée de Grenoble, 1936, cat. no. 155.

Provenance: Madame Edwards; F. & J. Tempelaere; G. Allard & Cie.; Madame R. Michel; Albert Dubosc à Saint Adresse.

GALERIE BRAME ET LORENCEAU, PARIS

CHILDE HASSAM (1859–1935)

Une Averse, Rue Bonaparte (Rainy Day, Rue Bonaparte)

American, 1887.

Signed, at lower left: CHILDE HASSAM 1887.

Oil on canvas; 40¼ × 77¼″ (102 × 196 cm).

Literature: Adeline Adams, *Childe Hassam*, New York, 1938, p. 34; Jules David Prown, *American Painting from Its Beginnings to the Armory Show*, Cleveland, 1969, p. 117, ill. p. 121; George M. Cohen, *A History of American Art*, New York, 1971, p. 151; Donaldson Hoops, *Childe Hassam*, New York, 1979, p. 26, ill. p. 27, pl. 3; William Gerdts, *American Impressionism*, Seattle, 1980, p. 58 (exhibition cat.); to be included in catalogue raisonné of the work of Childe Hassam, now being prepared by Stuart P. Feld.

Exhibitions: Paris Salon, 1887, no. 1181; Fifty-eighth Annual Exhibition, Pennsylvania Academy of the Fine Arts, Philadelphia, 1888, no. 156, p. 20; World's Columbian Exposition, Chicago, 1893, no. 536, (where it won a gold medal, as *Cab Station, Rue Bonaparte, Paris*); "Childe Hassam," Hirschl & Adler Galleries, New York, 1964, no. 6; "Childe Hassam: A Retrospective Exhibition," 1965, no. 6, p. 25, ill. p. 14 (exhibition seen at Corcoran Gallery of Art, Washington, D.C.; Museum of Fine Arts, Boston; Currier Gallery of Art, Manchester, New Hampshire; and The Museum of Modern Art, New York); "American Paintings for Public and Private Collections," Hirschl & Adler Galleries, 1967–1968, no. 46, ill.; "New York Collects," The Metropolitan Museum of Art, New York, 1968, no. 75, p. 12; "Impressionnistes Américains," 1982–1983, no. 24, ill. p. 28 (exhibition seen at the Petit Palais in Paris, East Berlin, Vienna, Bucharest, and Sofia).

Provenance: Mr. and Mrs. Thomas J. Wetzel, New York, until 1939; Milch Galleries, New York; Mr. Arthur D. Whiteside; Mr. and Mrs. Cecil Lipkin, until 1967; Private collection, New York, until 1978; Private collection, Wichita, Kansas.

HIRSCHL & ADLER GALLERIES, NEW YORK

JEAN BÉRAUD (1849–1936)

Champs Elysées with the Arc de Triomphe

French, c. 1890.

Signed, at lower right: JEAN BERAUD.

Oil on canvas; 22½ × 15¾″ (57 × 40 cm).

Provenance: Acquired in France by Mrs. Arthur Corwin, Greenwich, Connecticut; The Corwin Estate, Greenwich, Connecticut.

NEWHOUSE GALLERIES, INC., NEW YORK

**MARTIN JOHNSON HEADE
(1819–1904)**

New Jersey Marshes at Sunset

American, c. 1875

Signed, at lower left: M. J. HEADE

Oil on canvas; 13⅛ × 26⅛″ (33.5 × 66.5 cm).

Literature: Berry-Hill Galleries, Inc., New York, *American Painting 1850–1950*, 1981, p. 6, ill.

Provenance: Governor J. Proctor Knott, Kentucky; Private collection, New York.

**BERRY-HILL GALLERIES, INC.
NEW YORK**

HENRY F. FARNY (1847–1916)

Indian Encampment

American, c. 1890.

Signed and inscribed, at lower right: TO LIEUT. MORTON/IN FRIENDLY REMEMBRANCE OF/H. F. FARNY

Gouache on card; 15 × 29″ (38 × 73.5 cm).

Literature: Denny Carter, *Henry Farny*, New York, 1978, p. 199, ill.; Berry-Hill Galleries, Inc., New York, *American Paintings 1850–1950*, 1981, p. 32, ill.

Exhibitions: "Henry F. Farny," Whitney Gallery of Western Art, Cody, Wyoming, 1975; "Montana 1880–1910 with Henry Farny and Subjects," Charles Russell Museum, Great Falls, Montana, 1975 (ill. in catalogue as "Indian Camp").

Provenance: Mrs. Carnes Lee, whose husband, the late Colonel Carnes Lee, was aide-de-camp to General Morton from the mid-1920s until Lee's retirement.

BERRY-HILL GALLERIES, INC., NEW YORK

VINCENT VAN GOGH (1853–1890)

Head of a Peasant Woman with White Cap

Dutch, 1884.

Oil on canvas; 17¼ × 14½″ (43.5 × 37 cm).

Literature: J. B. de la Faille: *The Works of Vincent van Gogh*, Amsterdam, 1970 (orig. pub. Paris & Brussels, 1928), cat. no. 146a, ill.; *and Der Cicerone*, vol. XIX, 1927, ill. p. 102.

Provenance: Paul Schmolka, Prague–New York.

GALERIE NICOLINE PON, ZÜRICH

PAUL CÉZANNE (1839–1906)

Still Life

French, c. 1892.

Oil on canvas; 10½ × 14″ (26.5 × 35.5 cm)

Literature: To be recorded and illustrated by John Rewald in his forthcoming catalogue raisonné of Cézanne.

Provenance: Ambroise Vollard; purchased from Vollard in 1893 by Daniel Halevy, Paris; Leon Halevy, Paris.

STEPHEN HAHN, INC., NEW YORK

EGON SCHIELE (1890–1918)

Bekehrung (*Conversion*)

Austrian, 1912.

Signed and dated, at lower left: EGON SCHIELE 1912.

Oil on canvas; 27½ × 31½" (70 × 80 cm).

Exhibition: "Egon Schiele," Seibu Museum of Art, Tokyo, 1979, cat. no. 34, ill. on cover.

SERGE SABARSKY GALLERY, NEW YORK

TWENTIETH CENTURY

With Durand-Ruel, Agnew, and Knoedler this brief history of collecting and art dealing has reached the twentieth century. Why, one may ask, stop there? The explanation is simple. Today there are so many excellent and reliable dealers in art and in antiquities of all kinds that to mention one rather than another would be invidious. Collecting and art dealing have never flourished as they have in this century and particularly during the last two decades. Judging by the number of new museums, by prices of paintings, sculptures, and antiques, and by magazine articles and television shows, art, to quote Whistler, "is on the town" as never before. A description of the passionate, almost feverish, desire that has arisen to possess objects of beauty would require not an introduciton like this but a huge volume.

Over the years, what outstanding characteristics of dealers have emerged? One is certainly persuasiveness. Museum professionals depend on donations from private collectors more than on purchase funds for the enrichment of their institutions. Without the persuasiveness of dealers, very few of their collections would have been formed. As a former museum director I am particularly aware of this. How often have I tried to induce a collector to buy something needed for the National Gallery of Art—and failed, only to watch an able dealer convince the potential donor that the work of art is essential for his own collection and, through his generosity, might someday hang on the walls of the Gallery.

Auction houses have always been a source of sup-ply for art dealers, but in recent years they have also become dangerous competitors. The change occurred when Peter Wilson of Sotheby's decided his firm had not done enough to attract private collectors. With brochures, photographs, letters, and telephone calls, he managed to increase auction attendance. Henry Clay Frick, Joseph Widener, Isabella Gardner, the Havemeyers, Andrew Mellon, Samuel Kress, and other great collectors rarely bought at sales. Their purchases were from art dealers, and they were not troubled by the mark-up they paid. The increase was well worthwhile, they decided, because they could bring the works of art to their houses and live with them before deciding to buy. Museums, too, have always preferred to make their purchases from dealers rather than at auction, again because of the opportunity to have the painting, sculpture, or piece of furniture thoroughly studied at the museum.

Then for a collector there is also the pleasure of developing a rapport with a dealer; collectors and dealers have often become close friends. A collector can never become particularly attached to an auctioneer. Sentiment has no place in the auction room. Values determine the bids, unless someone succumbs to auction fever and bids too much. The transaction itself is a business, and logically auction houses have tried more and more to persuade their clients to regard their purchases as business investments. To a lover of art, this is a tragic development; it places the emphasis on money instead of on beauty. My grandfather, who was in business

CONTINUED ON PAGE 194

SCULPTURAL CANDELABRUM

Belgian, c. 1900, Art Nouveau.

Egide Rombaux (b. 1865), sculptor, and Franz Hoosemans, silversmith.

Ivory, silver; 14¼″ H (36 cm).

Similar examples: See Maurice Rheims, *L'objet 1900*, Paris, 1964, front cover, and Wolfgang Scheffler, *Werke um 1900*, Berlin, 1966, p. 17.

LILLIAN NASSAU LTD., NEW YORK

HAIR COMBS

French (Paris), c. 1900, Art Nouveau.

Blond tortoiseshell, pearls, opals, turquoise.

Far left, Lucien Gaillard (b. 1861), 4¾″ L (12 cm), signed: L. GAILLARD; second from left, Lucien Gaillard, 6″ L (15 cm), signed: L. GAILLARD; center,

Lucien Gaillard, 3½″ L (9 cm), signed: L. GAILLARD; second from right, Maison Vever, 6″ L (15 cm), signed: VEVER; far right, Maison Vever, 4½″ L (11.5 cm), signed: VEVER.

LILLIAN NASSAU LTD., NEW YORK

ORIENTAL RUG

Persian (Tabriz), 1900.

Wool; 108 × 79″ (274.5 × 200.5 cm).

The border contains scripts from Persian literature, and the central motif is a tree-of-life design.

A. BESHAR & COMPANY, INC., NEW YORK

ORIENTAL RUG

Caucasian (Kazak), 1906.

Wool; 59 × 43″ (150 × 109 cm).

The script on this prayer rug is translated, "Congratulations for Ramadan."

A. BESHAR & COMPANY, INC., NEW YORK

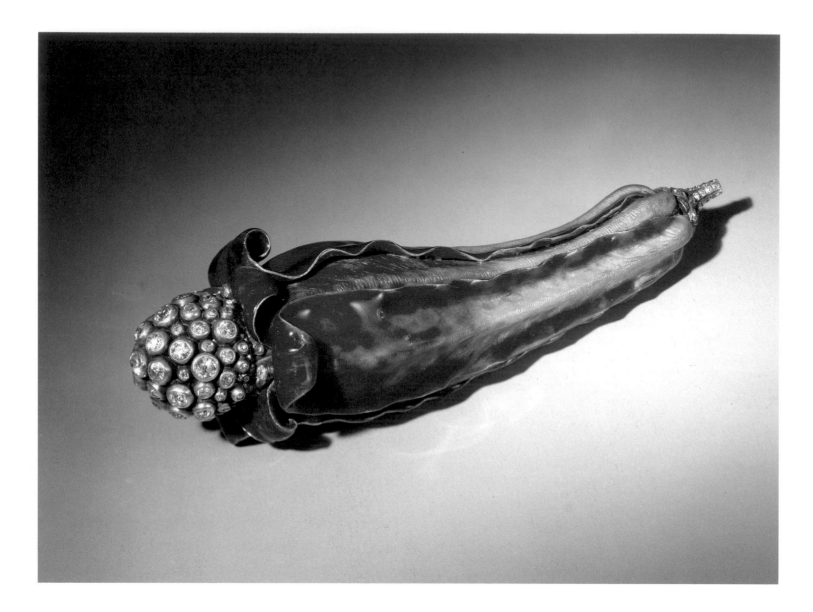

LILY-SHAPED PERFUME BOTTLE

American, c. 1900.

Designed by Louis Comfort Tiffany (1848–1933); executed by Julia Munson and sold by Tiffany & Co., New York.

Signed, on inside cover: TIFFANY & CO. NEW YORK.

Gold, diamonds, enamel; 4⅜″ L (11 cm).

LILLIAN NASSAU LTD., NEW YORK

PORTRAIT MINIATURE

Russian, c. 1900.

Made by the Fabergé firm under Chief Workmaster Henrik Wigström (1867–c. 1930). Signed FABERGÉ along with the initials of Wigström. Inscribed FLAME on frame.

Enameled gold, nephrite frame with gold inner border; 4⅛ × 4⅝″ (10.4 × 11.9 cm).

This portrait of the alert gun dog "Flame" at Sandringham is an example of Fabergé's monochrome enamel painting. It was likely part of a small group of miniatures that were the inspiration of H. C. Bainbridge, Fabergé's manager in London. There are similar works in the Queen's collection in London today.

WARTSKI, LONDON

with Henry Clay Frick, once told me that Frick took a surprising interest in what Velásquez had been paid for one of his portraits of Philip IV. The reason, Grandfather learned, was that his friend computed, at compound interest, the present rise in value of the picture. In the end, he was satisfied he had not paid too much. Frick, however, was a superb connoisseur, and it was the fascination of the portrait itself that stirred him. No great collector has ever bought for investment. Increase in value is generally a matter for dealers.

Until the Depression of 1929, most expensive works of art were bought by private collectors. As A. Hyatt Mayor has said, these men, "were often discriminating but felt comfortable with dealers who either made no parade of knowledge or, better, honestly did not know much. The decimation of fortunes in the crash opened the field for museum collecting." Confronted with curators rather than rich industrialists or stockbrokers, art dealers felt the need for further education. They attended university art courses to learn the jargon of experts, and they trained themselves to feel no inferiority before museum personnel. Consequently, the standards of scholarship among dealers have vastly increased.

Learned as they have become, art dealers continue to face a problem that affects auction houses much less—the mutability of fashion. If William Agnew had not managed to sell off his stock of paintings by artists like Herbert, Clarkson, Stanfield, T. S. Cooper, J. B. Pyne, Creswick, and others, he would have found himself stuck with pictures that today would be worthless. As his descendant, Geoffrey Agnew, has written, "A dealer can seldom afford to initiate taste, but a dealer with flair can anticipate the circumstances in which taste changes and by doing so accelerate that change." This is precisely what William Agnew did when he abandoned contemporary art for earlier painters. But this acceleration of change is related to another fact, which is not often mentioned: dealers may run out of stock of a particular period, as I have said, and then change becomes vital. Certain types of works of art cease to be available, such as major examples of Quattrocento art today. If a fine painting by Botticelli, Castagno, or Ghirlandaio is discovered, an event that occurs infrequently, it will inevitably be bought at an enormous price by a museum. For those particular Old Masters, private collectors are squeezed out of the market.

Moreover, so much research has been devoted to the most renowned Italian, Flemish, German, and Spanish masters that there is little original material left to be discovered. Meanwhile, hordes of young art historians are looking for subjects for their Ph.D. theses, and a revaluation occurs, so that painters and sculptors disdained a few years ago are now all the cry. John Addington Symonds wrote in 1886:

Perhaps a generation will yet arise which will take the Carracci and their scholars into favor. ... Whether the whirligig of time will bring about a revenge for the Eclectics yet remains to be seen. Taste is so capricious, or rather the conditions which create taste are so complex and inscrutable, that even this, which now seems impossible, may happen in the future. But a modest prediction can be hazarded that nothing short of the substitution of Catholicism for science and of Jesuitry for truth in the European mind will work a general revolution in their favor.

What Symonds thought only Catholicism and Jesuitry could do, Ph.D. candidates and dealers have done. At about the same time, but with more foresight, Léon Rosenthal wrote, "The day is not far off when we will find ourselves enthusing

CONTINUED ON PAGE 205

194

RECLINING CHAIR

Austrian (Vienna), 1905.

Designed by Josef Hoffmann (1870–1956); made by Kohn, Vienna.

Beechwood, bent and stained; 43 × 24½ × 32½″ (110 × 62 × 83 cm).

Literature: *Moderne Bauformen*, 7 Jahrgang, 1908, p. 370; Dorothy Müller, *Klassiker des Modernen Mobeldesign*, Munich, 1980, cover ill.; Daniele Baroni and Antonio D'Auria, *Josef Hoffmann and the Wiener Werkstätte*, Milan, 1981, cover ill., pp. 100–101; *Moderne Vergangenheit 1800–1900*, Vienna, 1981 (cat. from exhibition at Künstlerhaus, Vienna, May–August 1981, cf. p. 299, no. 233).

Exhibited: "Kunstschau," Schwartzenberg Platz, Vienna, 1908.

Provenance: Adrienne Gessner, Vienna.

GALERIE METROPOL, VIENNA

FREDERICK CARL FRIESEKE
(1874–1939)

Left: *Afternoon Tea on the Terrace*, oil on canvas, 55 × 56" (140 × 142 cm).

Right: *Windy Day on the Beach*, oil on canvas, 55 × 52" (140 × 132 cm).

American, 1906.

Literature: Tristan Leclère, "La Décoration d'un Hôtel Américain," *L'Art Décoratif*, July–December 1906, pp. 195–200.

Provenance: Shelburne Hotel, Atlantic City, New Jersey, 1906–1972.

In 1906, Rodman Wanamaker commissioned Frieseke to paint beach-scene murals for the Shelburne Hotel. These are two of seven paintings, all of which measure a total length of sixty feet, or twenty meters.

DAVID DAVID, INC.,
PHILADELPHIA

JOHN SINGER SARGENT
(1856–1925)

Portrait of Helen Brice

American, 1907.

Signed, at upper left: JOHN S. SARGENT.

Oil on canvas; 58 × 34″ (147 × 86 cm.)

Literature: Boston *Transcript*, 1914; William Howe Downes, *John S. Sargent, His Life and Work*, Boston, 1925, p. 230; David McKibbin, *Sargent's Boston*, Boston, 1956, p. 86; Charles M. Mount, *John Singer Sargent*, London, 1957, p. 349.

Exhibitions: Royal Academy, London, 1908; National Academy of Design, New York, 1908–1909; Venice Biennale, 1909, no. 35; Copley Society, Boston, 1914; Museum of Fine Arts, Boston, 1925, no. 98.

Provenance: Miss Helen Brice, New York; by family descent to Mrs. William Brice Hobbs, Connecticut (niece of sitter), until 1980.

IRA SPANIERMAN, INC., NEW YORK

**EDWARD LAMSON HENRY
(1841–1919)**

Von Steuben Tavern

American, 1909.

Signed, at lower right: E. L. HENRY.1909.

Oil on canvas; 17¼ × 32″ (44 × 81 cm).

Literature: Cragsmoor (New York) Free Library, *E. L. Henry's Country Life, An Exhibition*, 1981.

Exhibition: "E. L. Henry's Country Life, An Exhibition," 1981, sponsored jointly by the Cragsmoor Free Library and The New York State Museum.

FRANK S. SCHWARZ AND SON, PHILADELPHIA

FERNAND LÉGER (1881–1955)

Trois femmes (*Three Women*)

French, 1922.

Signed and dated, at lower right: F.L. 22.

Pencil on paper; 12 × 16½″ (30.5 × 42 cm).

Exhibition: "Drawings from Chicago Collections," Museum of Contem-porary Art, Chicago, September–November 1973.

Provenance: David Thompson, Falmouth, Massachusetts.

RICHARD GRAY GALLERY, CHICAGO

JOAN MIRÓ (b. 1893)

Été (*Summer*)

Spanish, 1929.

Signed on reverse: MIRO.

Paper collage with pen-and-pencil drawing; 25 × 38⅝″ (63.5 × 98 cm).

Literature: Jacques Dupin, *Joan Miró, Life and Work*, New York, 1962, p. 521, no. 253; Achille Bonito Oliva, *L'Imagine Stordita*, Rome, 1981, ill. in color.

Exhibition: "L'Imagine Stordita," Zwirner Gallery, Cologne, and Sprovieri, Rome, 1981.

Provenance: Galerie Pierre, Paris; Sam Kootz, New York; Private collection, New York; Galerie Thomas Borgmann.

RICHARD GRAY GALLERY, CHICAGO

ALEXEJ JAWLENSKY (1864–1941)

Roter Hut (Red Hat)

German, 1912.

Signed, at lower left: A JAWLENSKY.

Oil on board; 21 × 19½″ (53.5 × 49.5 cm).

SERGE SABARSKY GALLERY, NEW YORK

**ALBERTO GIACOMETTI
(1901–1966)**

Nu debout III (Standing Nude III)

Swiss-Italian, 1953.

Inscribed on base, at right side:
ALBERTO GIACOMETTI 1953.

Bronze, cast no. 4/6; 21½ × 4¾ ×
6¼″ (54.5 × 12 × 16 cm).

Literature: Guggenheim Museum,
New York, *Alberto Giacometti*, 1974,
p. 97, no. 67 (cast no. 1/6).

Provenance: Pierre Matisse; Leigh
Block.

**RICHARD GRAY GALLERY,
CHICAGO**

JEAN DUBUFFET (b. 1901)

La maison de campagne (*House in the Country*)

French, 1957.

Signed and dated, at lower right: J. DUBUFFET 57. Also inscribed and signed on reverse.

Oil on canvas; 35 × 45¾″ (89 × 116 cm).

Literature: *Catalogue des travaux de Jean Dubuffet*, Fascicule no. XIII (Célébration du sol I, lieux cursifs, texturologies, topographies), Lausanne, 1969, p. 55, no. 70, ill.

Provenance: Galerie de Clos de Sierne, Geneva.

RICHARD GRAY GALLERY, CHICAGO

over...those depressing Bolognese whom we loved yesterday and whom we will love again tomorrow." The smart picture or antiques dealer must anticipate such changes and assemble a stock of the latest fashion, be it in Old Masters or decorative arts.

Since supplies of available Old Masters, except for Baroque paintings, have dried up, drained by museum collections and private purchases, more and more dealers have turned to the unstable market of contemporary painting. Some guarantee a certain sum of money annually to those artists whose work they admire. (This system goes back at least to the eighteenth century. Consul Smith, the "Merchant of Venice," as Walpole called him, employed Canaletto to paint exclusively for him at a fixed price for a certain number of years.) Supporting an artist is more complicated than it may seem on the surface, as Maurice Rheims points out in his admirable book, *The Art Market*. Rheims describes how an artist may have been working for years and may have exhausted his means. The dozen or so canvases that he may sell annually—and only then if he is lucky—do not provide enough money for studio rent and painting materials. One day an adventuresome dealer offers him a one-year contract. The dealer will pay the artist an allowance, for which the painter will provide the dealer with a fixed number of pictures. The sum agreed on is usually less than a day laborer would earn. Nevertheless, the dealer is not exploiting the artist because he is faced with the expense of an exhibition, invitations, publicity, a catalogue. He knows that the show will probably be a failure, but there is the chance of success. The prices of the pictures are low, and the dealer's clients, who have usually taken his advice, buy all the paintings. The buyers then become the artist's publicity agents, showing his pictures to their friends and saying how clever the dealer has been to discover a new genius.

Then, Rheims continues, a critical situation arises.

The friends rush to buy the artist's pictures, and the dealer feels he must increase prices fourfold. The painter's contract is at an end, and other dealers are bidding for him. Determined to make as much as he can, the artist increases his output tremendously, and the dealer is now confronted with the task of maintaining the value of a large number of pictures, a difficult job. The dealer must increase publicity, arrange for articles, prepare elaborate catalogues with introductions by distinguished writers, and do everything possible to see that the next vernissage will sell out. The painter has become as famous as a movie star, and his work is considered a sound investment. In the past, people might have purchased his pictures for the sheer pleasure of hanging them on the wall, but now they regard the work as valuable shares of stock. The dealer can't sell his artist short, as he might well wish to do. He is required to maintain the high prices. This means bidding up his painter's work whenever his pictures are sold at auction, a constant peril, for he must protect his clients and sustain his reputation as a sound source of art investment. He has become the equivalent of a stockbroker, without wishing to be.

This sad development, encouraged by bankers and investment houses, has become ubiquitous. Even the viewers who come to this exhibition may regard the works of art they see as sources of potential profit. I hope this will not be their attitude. Instead, I trust visitors will consider these items as a showcase of many of the finest works of art now for sale and that they will appreciate each piece for its own beauty. In spite of the way museums, like highly charged magnets, pull masterpieces from the market, never allowing them to return, it is extraordinary that there still remain so many astoundingly lovely objects.

For more than twenty centuries, a monetary value has been attributed to art treasures by collectors, dealers, even museums. Much as one may deplore this economic fact, the preciousness of these works in terms of hard cash, of gold, has often protected them from destruction by those who may be indifferent to their intrinsic beauty, like the Roman general Lucius Mummius at Corinth. Through wars and revolutions, lovers of art have tried to give shelter and sanctuary to these witnesses to human genius. They have faced death, as did Gaius Verres for his Corinthian bronzes, and only approaching death, as we have seen, compelled Mazarin to release his hold on his beautiful possessions.

When works of art reenter the market, usually through adverse circumstances or death, they are acquired and passed on to others. Sometimes their new owners value them only for their monetary worth, but often their possessors become lovers of the beautiful. These enlightened collectors recognize that they are custodians of part of our human heritage, and that it is their duty to hand this on to the future. Thus one may hope that art will be enjoyed from generation to generation. As we have seen, history indicates that there will always be those who cherish and protect beauty so long as our planet is inhabitable. This, we can only pray, will be true for some time to come.

John Walker, Director Emeritus
National Gallery of Art, Washington, D.C.
Easter Barton, Amberley, Arundel
West Sussex, May 1982

206

ACKNOWLEDGMENTS

When I was asked to write this essay, I assumed it would be easy to find books on the history of art dealing and of collecting. I was mistaken. So far as I know, there is no book that tells the story of the sale of works of art over the centuries, and the formation of collections is dealt with fragmentarily in many places. There have been, however, six books I have used extensively, and to their authors and editors I am deeply indebted:

Joseph Alsop. *The Rare Art Traditions*. New York, Harper & Row, 1982.

Samuel P. Avery. *The Diaries 1871–1882 of Samuel P. Avery, Art Dealer*. Ed. by Madeleine Fidell Beaufort, Herbert L. Kleinfield, Jeanne J. Welcher. Foreword by A. Hyatt Mayor. New York, Arno Press, 1979.

W. Buchanan. *Memoirs of Painting*. London, Ackerman, 1824.

Francis Haskell. *Rediscoveries in Art*. London, Phaedon, 1976.

Maurice Rheims. *Art on the Market, Midas to Getty*. London, Weidenfeld & Nicolson, 1961.

Francis Henry Taylor. *The Taste of Angels*. Boston, Little, Brown and Company, 1948.

I must also mention two books compiled by the firms in question:

Agnew's 1817–1967. London, The Bradbury Agnew Press Ltd., 1967.

Colnaghi's 1760–1960. London, privately published, 1960.

I have had to read many articles, far too many, but I list only those that have been the most helpful:

Geoffrey de Bellaigue. "George IV and the Arts of France," *Antiques*, May 1966.

Lorne Campbell. "The Art Market in the Southern Netherlands," *Burlington*, April 1976.

J. F. Hayward. "Jacopo da Strada, XVI Century Antique Dealer," *Art at Auction, 1971–1972*, New York, 1973.

Frank Herrman, "Who Was Solly?" *The Connoisseur*, in five parts beginning April 1967.

A. Hyatt Mayor. "Remembrance of Dealers Past," *ARTnews*, October 1974.

John Walsh, "Vermeer," *Bulletin of The Metropolitan Museum of Art*, Summer 1973.

W. L. van de Watering, introduction to *A Collector's Choice*, an exhibition at the Mauritshuis, The Hague, 1982.

I would like to say a word about the assistance I have received from Patricia Bayer, Projects Coordinator of C.I.N.O.A. She helped me find many articles, far beyond the number listed in the bibliography; and she photostated those not available in London. Without her help this essay could not have been written.

LIST OF EXHIBITORS
Numbers indicate page references.

A La Vieille Russie, Inc.
781 Fifth Avenue
New York, New York 10022, U.S.A.
Pp. 73, 118, 119, 143, 171

Didier Aaron, Inc.
32 East 67th Street
New York, New York 10021, U.S.A.
Also at: 32, avenue Raymond-Poincaré
75116 Paris, France

9002 Melrose Avenue
Los Angeles, California 90069, U.S.A.
Pp. 56, 86, 130, 131

Gemäldegalerie Abels
Stadtwaldgürtel 32 A
5000 Cologne 41, West Germany
Pp. 122—123, 148

Arthur Ackermann & Son Ltd.
3, Old Bond Street
London W1X 3TD, England
P. 101

Galerie Jacques Barrère
36, rue Mazarine
75006 Paris, France
P. 21

Berry-Hill Galleries, Inc.
743 Fifth Avenue
New York, New York 10022, U.S.A.
Pp. 162, 177, 182, 183

A. Beshar & Company, Inc.
49 East 53rd Street
New York, New York 10022, U.S.A.
Pp. 190, 191

Vojtech Blau Inc.
800-B Fifth Avenue
New York, New York 10021, U.S.A.
Pp. 33, 167

Blumka Gallery
949 Park Avenue
New York, New York 10028, U.S.A.
P. 36

Julius Böhler
Pacellistrasse 8/II
8000 Munich 2, West Germany
P. 108

Galerie Brame et Lorenceau
68, boulevard Malesherbes
75008 Paris, France
Pp. 156, 179

Bresset
5, quai Voltaire
75007 Paris, France
P. 26

Arthur Brett and Sons Limited
42, St. Giles Street
Norwich NR2 1LW, England
P. 44

Cailleux
136, faubourg Saint-Honoré
75008 Paris, France
P. 78

Ralph M. Chait Galleries, Inc.
12 East 56th Street
New York, New York 10022, U.S.A.
Pp. 12, 13, 68, 69, 165

Philip Colleck of London Ltd.
122 East 57th Street
New York, New York 10022, U.S.A.
P. 96

M. Darling Limited
250 Mercer Street, Mercer Square B707
New York, New York 10012, U.S.A.
P. 74

Dalva Brothers, Inc.
44 East 57th Street
New York, New York 10022, U.S.A.
Pp. 63, 82, 138, 139, 140

David David, Inc.
260 South 18th Street
Philadelphia, Pennsylvania 19103, U.S.A.
Pp. 196–197

Jan Dirven
Keizersgracht 15
5611 GC Eindhoven, The Netherlands
Pp. 20, 24

R.H. Ellsworth Ltd.
960 Fifth Avenue
New York, New York 10021, U.S.A.
P. 16

Fabius Frères
152, boulevard Haussmann
75008 Paris, France
P. 147

Richard L. Feigen & Co.
113 East 79th Street
New York, New York 10021, U.S.A.
Pp. 124–125, 158–159, 160

Firestone & Parson Ltd., Inc.
Ritz Carlton
Boston, Massachusetts 02117, U.S.A.
P. 146

Fleur-de-Lis Antiques
309 South County Road
Palm Beach, Florida 33480, U.S.A.
P. 152

E & J Frankel Ltd. Oriental Art
25 East 77th Street
New York, New York 10021, U.S.A.
Pp. 15, 141

Price Glover, Inc.
57 East 57th Street
New York, New York 10022, U.S.A.
Pp. 90, 99

Lucien Goldschmidt, Inc.
1117 Madison Avenue
New York, New York 10028, U.S.A.
P. 80

F. Gorevic & Son, Inc.
660 Lexington Avenue
New York, New York 10022, U.S.A.
Pp. 144, 164, 173

Richard Gray Gallery
620 North Michigan Avenue
Chicago, Illinois 60611, U.S.A.
Pp. 200, 201, 203, 204

Richard Green (Fine Paintings)
44, Dover Street
London W1X 4JQ, England
Also at: 4, New Bond Street
    London W1Y 9PE, England
Pp. 55, 76

Stephen Hahn, Inc.
9 East 79th Street
New York, New York 10021, U.S.A.
Pp. 168, 185

Hirschl & Adler Galleries, Inc.
21 East 70th Street
New York, New York 10021, U.S.A.
Pp. 178, 180

Galerie Hoogsteder
Surinamestraat 26
The Hague, The Netherlands
Pp. 34–35

Bernard Houthakker C.V.
Rokin 98
1012 KZ Amsterdam, The Netherlands
P. 40

H.G. Klein
St. Apernstrasse 2
5000 Cologne 1, West Germany
Pp. 31, 42, 43

D.S. Lavender (So. Molton Antiques Ltd.)
63, South Molton Street
London W1Y 1HH, England
Pp. 111, 132

Ronald A. Lee (Fine Arts) Ltd.
1-9, Bruton Place
London W1, England
P. 38

Bernard & S. Dean Levy, Inc.
981 Madison Avenue
New York, New York 10021, U.S.A.
P. 128

Étienne Lévy
178, faubourg Saint-Honoré
75008 Paris, France
Pp. 114, 115

Meinz-Arnold
Baurs Park 21
2000 Hamburg, Blankenese, W. Germany
P. 72

Galerie Bruno Meissner
Bahnhofstrasse 14
8001 Zürich, Switzerland
P. 53

Galerie Metropol
Dorotheergasse 12
1010 Vienna, Austria
Also at: 927 Madison Avenue
    New York, New York 10021, U.S.A.
P. 195

Joseph M. Morpurgo
108 Rokin
1012 LA Amsterdam, The Netherlands
P. 48

Galerie Müllenmeister
Pfaffenberger Weg 87
5650 Solingen, West Germany
Pp. 50, 51

Fred B. Nadler Antiques, Inc.
67 Mount Street, P.O. Box 97
Bay Head, New Jersey 08742, U.S.A.
Also at: P.O. Box 558, Lenox Hill Station
    New York, New York 10021, U.S.A.
Pp. 102, 103

Lillian Nassau Ltd.
220 East 57th Street
New York, New York 10022, U.S.A.
Pp. 174, 175, 188, 189, 192

Neuse-Antiquitäten
Am Wall 153/56
2800 Bremen 1, West Germany
Pp. 25, 27, 91, 121

Newhouse Galleries, Inc.
19 East 66th Street
New York, New York 10021, U.S.A.
Pp. 150, 181

S. Nijstad Oude Kunst B.V.
Ruychrocklaan 442
2597 EJ The Hague, The Netherlands
P. 59

Noortman & Brod, Ltd.
24, St. James's Street
London SW1A 1HA, England
Also at: 8, Bury Street
    St. James's
    London SW1Y 6AB, England

    1020 Madison Avenue
    New York, New York 10021, U.S.A.

    Vrijthof, 49
    Maastricht, The Netherlands
P. 61

Florian Papp, Inc.
962 Madison Avenue
New York, New York 10021, U.S.A.
P. 116

Peters' Oude Kunst B.V.
Spoorlan 438
5038 CH Tilburg, The Netherlands
P. 88

S. J. Phillips Ltd.
139, New Bond Street
London W1A 3DL, England
Pp. 71, 110, 120

Galerie Nicoline Pon
Spiegelgasse 13
8001 Zürich, Switzerland
P. 184

G. Randall Fine Antiques & Works of Art
229 North Royal Street
Alexandria, Virginia 22314, U.S.A.
Pp. 83, 84, 94, 97, 98

William Redford
9, Mount Street
London W1Y 5AD, England
P. 134

Gerhard Röbbig
Kardinal-Faulhaber-Strasse 15
8000 Munich 2, West Germany
Pp. 92, 93, 104, 107

James Robinson Inc.
15 East 57th Street
New York, New York 10022, U.S.A.
Pp. 37, 79, 154, 170, 172

Paul Rosenberg & Co.
20 East 79th Street
New York, New York 10021, U.S.A.
Pp. 57, 87, 133

Rosenberg & Stiebel, Inc.
32 East 57th Street
New York, New York 10022, U.S.A.
Pp. 18, 23, 65, 117, 137

Serge Sabarsky Gallery
987 Madison Avenue
New York, New York 10021, U.S.A.
Pp. 186, 202

Israel Sack, Inc.
15 East 57th Street
New York, New York 10022, U.S.A.
P. 127

Spencer A. Samuels & Co., Ltd.
13 East 76th Street
New York, New York 10021, U.S.A.
Pp. 30, 58, 64

Kunsthandel Xaver Scheidwimmer
Ottostrasse 3
8000 Munich 2, West Germany
Pp. 66, 67

Otto Schmitt
Frankenwerft 35-Fischmarkt
5000 Cologne 1, West Germany
P. 22

Frank S. Schwarz and Son
1806 Chestnut Street
Philadelphia, Pennsylvania 19103, U.S.A.
P. 199

M. & G. Ségal
Aeschengraben 14
4051 Basel, Switzerland
P. 112

Maurice Segoura Gallery
20, faubourg Saint-Honoré
75008 Paris, France
Also at: 58 East 79th Street
    New York, New York 10021, U.S.A.
P. 100

Matthew & Elisabeth Sharpe
Spring Mill
Conshohocken, Pennsylvania 19428, U.S.A.
P. 105

H. Shickman Gallery
1000 Park Avenue
New York, New York 10028, U.S.A.
Pp. 52, 54, 136

S. J. Shrubsole Corp.
104 East 57th Street
New York, New York 10022, U.S.A.
P. 145

S. J. Shrubsole, Ltd.
43, Museum Street
London WC1A 1LY, England
P. 70

Wolfgang A. Siedler
Himmelpfortgasse 15
1010 Vienna, Austria
P. 29

Ira Spanierman, Inc.
50 East 78th Street
New York, New York 10021, U.S.A.
P. 198

Edward Speelman Ltd.
Empire House
175, Piccadilly
London W1V 0NP, England
P. 109

Spink & Son Ltd.
5, 6 & 7 King Street
St. James's
London SW1Y 6QS, England
P. 10

Stair & Co., Inc.
59 East 57th Street
New York, New York 10022, U.S.A.

Also at: 10900 Wilshire Boulevard
   Los Angeles, California 90024, U.S.A.

120, Mount Street
London W1Y 5HB, England
P. 166

Garrick C. Stephenson
50 East 57th Street
New York, New York 10022, U.S.A.
Pp. 46, 47, 95

David Stockwell, Inc.
3701 Kennett Pike, P. O. Box 3840
Wilmington, Delaware 19807, U.S.A.
Pp. 126, 129

E. V. Thaw & Co., Inc.
726 Park Avenue
New York, New York 10021, U.S.A.
P. 169

David Tunick, Inc.
12 East 81st Street
New York, New York 10028, U.S.A.
P. 60

Earle D. Vandekar of Knightsbridge, Inc.
15 East 57th Street
New York, New York 10022, U.S.A.
Also at: 138, Brompton Road
   London SW3 1HY, England
Pp. 113, 151

Vernay & Jussel, Inc.
825 Madison Avenue
New York, New York 10021, U.S.A.
P. 62

Frederick P. Victoria & Son, Inc.
154 East 55th Street
New York, New York 10022, U.S.A.
Pp. 106, 135, 142

Wartski
14, Grafton Street
London W1X 3LA, England
P. 193

ASSOCIATIONS AFFILIATED WITH C.I.N.O.A.

AUSTRIA

Bundesgremium des Handels mit Juwelen, Gold-,
Silberwaren, Uhren, Gemälden, Antiquitäten,
Kunstgegenständen und Briefmarken
Bauernmarkt 13
A-1010 Vienna

Erich Göschl, President

BELGIUM

Chambre des Antiquaires de Belgique
27, rue Ernest-Allard
B-1000 Brussels

Christian de Bruyn, President

DENMARK

Dansk Antikvitetshandler Union
Larsbjørnstræde 6
DK-1454 Copenhagen K

Ingvar Svensson, President

FRANCE

Chambre Syndicale de l'Estampe, du Dessin et du Tableau
117, boulevard Saint-Germain
75006 Paris

Robert Guiot, President

Syndicat National des Antiquaires, Négociants en Objets
d'Art, Tableaux Anciens et Modernes
11, rue Jean-Mermoz
75008 Paris

Philippe Brame, President

GERMANY

Bundesverband des Deutschen Kunst- und Antiquitäten-
handels
Stadtwaldgürtel 32 A
D-5000 Cologne 41

Günther Abels, President

GREAT BRITAIN

The British Antique Dealers' Association
20, Rutland Gate
London SW7 1BD

Charles Lee, President

The Society of London Art Dealers
38, Bury Street
London SW1Y 6BB

John Baskett, President

IRELAND

The Irish Antique Dealers' Association
27, St. Anne Street
Dublin 2

Ronald McDonnell, President

ITALY

Associazione Antiquari d'Italia
Lungarno Soderini 5
Florence

Giuseppe Bellini, President

Federazione Italiana Mercanti d'Arte
Corso Venezia 47–49
Milan

G. Mazzoleni, President

THE NETHERLANDS

Vereeniging van Handelaren in Oude Kunst in Nederland
Keizersgracht 207
1016 DS Amsterdam

D. R. Aronson, President

NEW ZEALAND

The New Zealand Antique Dealers' Association
99, Shortland Street
Auckland 3

Philip Rhodes, President

SOUTH AFRICA

The South African Antique Dealers' Association
Box 55020
Northlands 2116

P. Visser, President

SWITZERLAND

Kunsthandelsverband der Schweiz
Laupenstrasse 41
CH-3008 Bern

Eberhard W. Kornfeld, President

Verband Schweizerischer Antiquare und Kunsthändler
(Syndicat Suisse des Antiquaires et Commerçants d'Art)
Schachenstrasse 23
CH-4562 Biberist

André Kurmann, President

UNITED STATES

The Art and Antique Dealers League of America, Inc.
353 East 53rd Street
New York, New York 10022

David L. Dalva II, President

Art Dealers Association of America, Inc.
575 Madison Avenue
New York, New York 10022

Norman S. Hirschl, President

The National Antique & Art Dealers Association of
    America, Inc.
15 East 57th Street
New York, New York 10022

Peter L. Schaffer, President

C.I.N.O.A. ADMINISTRATION

President: Gerald G. Stiebel

Vice President: Edward Munves, Jr.

Secretary General: David L. Dalva II

Treasurer: Peter L. Schaffer

Councillor: Georges Baptiste

Directors: Christian de Bruyn
Stephen Hahn

Permanent Councillors: Giuseppe Bellini
Emile Bourgey
Jean Cailleux
Andrew Hill
Henry W. Rubin
Pierre Vandermeersch

Projects Coordinator: Patricia Bayer
Legal Counsel: William D. Zabel

Address: 32 East 57th Street
New York, New York 10022

Composition in Baskerville
by U.S. Lithograph Inc., New York, New York
Printing in four-color offset on 128 gsm matte-coated paper
by Toppan Printing Co., Ltd., Tokyo, Japan.
Bound in Japan by Toppan Printing Co., Ltd.